SOCIAL STUDIES SOURCES

Erling M. Hunt, Series Editor

**Congress and the President:
Readings in Executive-Legislative Relations**
by Walter Earl Travis

A Bibliography for Teachers of Social Studies
by Raymond A. Ducharme, Jr., Joseph Katz, and
Arthur D. Sheekey

Honors Teaching in American History
by Lawrence A. Fink

American History Through Conflicting Interpretations
by David F. Kellum

Charles A. Beard and the Social Studies: A Book of Readings
by Raymond A. Ducharme, Jr.

AMERICAN HISTORY THROUGH CONFLICTING INTERPRETATIONS

DAVID F. KELLUM

Social Studies Sources
Erling M. Hunt, Series Editor

Teachers College Press
Teachers College, Columbia University
New York, New York

Acknowledgments

I should like to acknowledge with gratitude the debt owed to two former teachers and colleagues of mine at Columbia Teachers College, Dr. Frederick D. Kershner, Jr. who planted the seeds from which this approach to teaching has sprung, and Dr. Erling M. Hunt, who directed its growth with wisdom and patience. I should like, at the same time, to absolve both from responsibility for whatever corruption of their ideas may have occurred in the shaping of the final product.

I would acknowledge too my debt to those at Teachers College Press for their patience, thoroughness, and great kindness in readying the manuscript for publication; and as well to the several publishing houses for their permission to make use of excerpts from publications of their own.

Finally I acknowledge a debt to my wife, Chrissie, for the checking of endless source lists, for her encouragement, long suffering, and love.

D. F. K.

Foreword

American history should be, above all, a continuing challenge of deepening interest—raising new questions for Americans and calling for varied, often controversial, answers. As the subject is usually presented, in a succession of factual summaries, it has become for students a conventional, bland, unstimulating, and, in fact, unrealistic account to be memorized. In skimming the surface of major movements and avoiding controversy, textbooks and courses in the main present students with neither the motivation nor the opportunity to move into primary sources and to challenge and discuss the differing interpretations of our past. Yet controversy has characterized American history from its beginnings. Historians have never agreed about causes, effects, leaders, or, in some cases, even about the events of our past.

Since World War II, a publishing revolution has made available in paperback collections of selected readings from sources as well as other volumes incorporating the changing and conflicting interpretations of historians. It is now more possible than ever before to involve youth in the essence of American history—in the controversies of establishing policies, in the controversies of applying them, and in the controversies of evaluating them retrospectively with their associated events, movements, and meanings. With such an approach to American history, individual investigation can replace passive memorization.

Dr. Kellum, an experienced teacher of high school and college students and of teachers of history themselves, offers one promising approach to vitalizing the study of a subject that in its nature overflows with vitality. His nine topics offer an acceptable alternative to the traditional survey for teachers who sense the need for and possibilities of an alternative. Or, for the less venturesome, they offer the possibility of combining study of a few of the topics with a predominantly survey course. Or for teachers who either like to make their own selection of topics or who differ from Dr. Kellum's choices, they offer both a pattern and some organizational and bibliographical help.

No program for teaching American history can or should satisfy all teachers, all classes, all situations. But the importance of our past, the restiveness of youth, and the availability of new instructional resources call for some such active and individual involvement of youth in the learning process as the interpretations approach proposes.

ERLING M. HUNT

Contents

One: The Purposes of Teaching American History in the High School

The conventional survey of American history offered in high schools (and colleges) across the nation is obsolete and has been so for a good many years. Yet the approach persists, and today, probably in most American history classrooms, the course emphasis is still placed upon coverage. From a theoretical standpoint, the validity of coverage as a course objective has always been open to question; from a practical standpoint, coverage is no longer possible within either a one-year or a two-year framework. To rescue the high school and college American history course calls for a substitution of depth for the superficial, self-defeating consideration of breadth.

The discussion that follows will indicate the comparative strengths and weaknesses of two quite different approaches to the teaching of American history: the conventional survey and the proposed interpretations approach. The interpretations approach comprises a carefully structured examination of a series of questions that demonstrate conflicting interpretations of selected major developments in American history. In resolving the conflict, the student is directed to authoritative secondary works and to primary sources. Prescribed lines of related investigation then continually open out from the central question; in effect, a problems approach with the "problem" being the resolution of conflicting interpretations of an historical development.

REQUIREMENTS OF SCHOLARSHIP

"Stubborn and irreducible" is the phrase borrowed by Charles Austin Beard to describe the three factors that condition the purposes of social studies instruction: ". . . the spirit and letter of scholarship . . . the realities and ideas of society in which it is carried on, and . . . the nature and limitations of the teaching and learning process. . . ." [1] This discussion will undertake to consider the purposes of teaching American history as suggested by two of Beard's irreducible factors—scholarship and social realities. Consideration of the nature and limitation of the teaching and learning process is the task of Chapter IV.

1

The debate persists among academicians concerned with scholarship as to whether the dissemination of information, the inculcation of understandings, or the development of skills is the primary purpose for the teaching of American history at the high school level. The debate often obscures the fact of unanimous agreement upon the importance of all three aims, in their mutually dependent relationship, to any study of history that pretends to achieve real value. Shifts in emphasis upon one aim or another are much in evidence in the history of teaching social studies in the United States, and have generally reflected major changes in the values of the society. The appearance and decline of the source method of teaching high school history in the closing decades of the nineteenth century[2] is one example of continuing evaluation and re-evaluation of the priority of purposes, but regardless of the recurrent innovations as to place of emphasis, no one of the three purposes, if the other two are ignored, can achieve the values of historical study.

INFORMATION

The imparting of information is so fundamental a purpose for teaching history that the necessity for actually doing so is in continual danger of being overlooked. It may be forgotten by those who are anxious to jump to the more personally satisfying work of developing understandings, a process which, however exasperating the fact may be, depends upon command of information. The necessity is also in danger of being overlooked by those who, oblivious to the need for information as a basis for understanding, reason that the mastering of factual detail which is readily available in books cannot be adequately justified even as a device for the development of a habit of accuracy. Another alternative, more stimulating to the teacher than concentration upon factual information, which becomes tedious, is the approach through historical method. But a preoccupation with historical method reaches a point where the pursuit of historical fact becomes more important than its attainment; it dictates the need, in teaching skills at the high school level, to focus main attention on the goal to which the skills lead—historical intelligence. Though no course can be developed solely upon the imparting of information, it is the foundation upon which every science or study rests. There is no proceeding to any more exalted purpose without first securing a substantial base. The classroom teacher must determine how this is to be done.

The survey approach to American history teaching focuses upon developing command of factual data. It often purports, to be sure, to develop understandings by organizing facts topically, by asserting cause-and-effect relationships, and by assuming that the result is explanation of the past. Historians have sharply challenged the assumption, noting the arbitrary selecting of the facts presented and the contrived identifying of the relationships imposed.[3] The result is bad history. The survey approach, unlike the interpretations approach, does not have any intrinsic power of generating interest in historical information. It does not provide a necessity for distinguishing between significant and non-significant information, nor does it include a means for demonstrating the value of the information since it makes no use of it. Professor Gilbert Highet captures the problem picturesquely:

> There is a story that Caffarelli, the eunuch who became one of finest sopranos of the baroque age, was tutored by a single faultless but relentless Italian master, who kept him at one single page of exercises for five years, and then dismissed him, saying "You may go: you are the greatest singer in Europe." Certainly the unhappy creature became one of the finest singers in history. He could sing melodies more purely and sweetly, and execute difficult runs more flexibly and gracefully, than any modern opera star. But his teacher took a chance which was quite unwarrantable, and which might not have succeeded with anyone except a eunuch. Most pupils, all pupils but a very few, would have demanded proof of their progress, in the shape of new assignments, fresh challenges, a change of any kind. Disciplined monotony is good training, but it easily becomes mechanical repetition; and by mechanical repetition nothing higher than card-tricks and juggling can ever (with the rarest and most laborious exceptions) be learnt or taught.[4]

The interpretations approach has the advantage of clearly demonstrating of itself the value of historical information. Data is not doled to the student in the largest portions that can be "learned" at one sitting; rather it is released to him through his own effort to find and make use of it. He is led to the information because he needs it; thus he discovers the information and is aware of its importance at the same time. The interpretations approach, or any problems approach, has a major advantage over the survey in that once the challenges are established and functioning, the need for facts is self-feeding and independent of any necessity for demonstrating the importance of the information by an outside agent. It accords with twentieth century historians who recognize multiple causation and the necessity for taking account of differing—even conflicting—interpretations of events in the past.[5]

UNDERSTANDINGS

Henry Johnson views the development of critical skills and of understandings as the major educational benefits that derive from the study of history: "There are two things that stand out as unique," he con-

3

tends: "(1) the historical method of arriving at facts; (2) the historical idea of development." [6] He further suggests that the historical idea of development forms the basis of our understanding of change, and that it is in providing this understanding, which consists of reasoning about the present from facts related to the past, that the study of history demonstrates its functional nature.

The question of which approach to history best satisfies the purpose of promoting an understanding of the value of history is hopelessly entangled in the controversy over what history's value is. While the importance of the general understanding of the nature of change is important, does the specific application of a study of the past to the present have relevance? Professor Michael Oakeshott suggests that the value of history is quite different:

> History is the product of a temperament that delights in the past, and for which the detachment, the immobility, the deadness and irrelevance of the past are not defects to be removed, but blessed virtues to be enjoyed. . . . The world has no love for what is dead, wishing only to recall it to life again and make it appear relevant to present pursuits and enterprises. It deals with the past as with a man, expecting it to talk sense and to have something apposite to say. But for the "historian" for whom the past is dead and irreproachable, the past is feminine. He loves it as a mistress of whom he never tires, and whom he never expects to talk sense.[7]

For the antiquarian, who finds "history for history's sake" a sufficient excuse for its study, who does not seek answers, whose interest is not in sifting and evaluating evidence for its uses in illuminating the present, either approach would be satisfying, but he would probably express a preference for the survey because, in permitting more time for narrative, it admits of greater possibilities for leisurely, non-purposeful spellbinding:

> History that traces development inevitably includes facts not directly related to the present. Its fundamental question is not what matters *now* but what mattered *then*. Its primary mission is to exhibit life as it *was* and to show what the things *were* that shaped *past* living. Even scientific history, however, reflects the tastes, interests, and problems of the present in which it is written, and, as organized for schools, is as deeply concerned with the present as the functional approach. In much of actual content it is in fact so largely shaped by the present that, like the history shaped by the functional approach, it is constantly going out of date.[8]

For the "functionalist," anxious to turn up things of the past which he feels will illuminate the future, the interpretations approach or any approach that similarly emphasizes skills, and that invests the subject matter with an utilitarian importance, more adequately serves the purpose of promoting an understanding of the value of history.

Emphasizing the value of understanding subject matter relationships and present-day applications of a study of the past, Jacques Barzun states:

> What history teaches . . . is not the date of the Monroe Doctrine—that is incidental—but how such a document can come into being, why the British Navy was necessary to its effectiveness, how its meaning has changed, and what involvements of life and death may yet hang upon it.[9]

For the purpose of conveying an understanding of the nature of history the interpretations approach is the better suited. Here history is introduced and studied in terms of its complexity, focusing student attention upon its depth while the picture of history posed by the survey is one of simplicity, inviting the student's attention rather to its breadth. The survey inclines toward fixing positions in terms of the known, whereas the interpretations approach directs attention to uncertainty: to changing analyses, re-consideration, re-evaluation, re-interpretation —the composite of flux.

A final consideration of the understandings advanced by each of the two approaches concerns the perspective of history, the proper understanding of which requires appreciation both of its expanse and of the point that not all events and dates are of equal significance. The process of selection serves as an important index to what is, at least in the opinion of some authorities, more significant. The survey approach, with its greater range, is less obviously selective in its subject matter presentation. In its process of selection, however, the interpretations approach clearly identifies particular developments as being of particular significance.

The survey approach inclines toward smothering distinction; the interpretations approach risks overdrawing significance. Lacking a broad base at the start, the student in a survey rarely can be brought to an understanding of the whole after an introduction to the rapid succession of its parts.

SKILLS

Herbert Baxter Adams is quoted as having written in 1879 that "It is, perhaps, of as much consequence to teach a young person *how* to study history as to teach him history itself." [10] Professor Henry Johnson has stressed the importance of developing the skill of critical thinking,[11] and more recently, Professor Erling M. Hunt has written: "Education that implements democratic ideals must be practical and realistic, must deal with issues that are current and controversial, must avoid teaching *what* to think and emphasize *how* to think." [12] In the teaching of American history the necessity for developing skills, reading, writing, and particularly critical thinking, has been a recurring theme, and the importance of all three to the democratic political society should be immediately evident.

Because the survey of history emphasizes content, it is not as adequately suited to satisfying the purpose of developing skills as is the interpretations approach, which embodies the critical treatment of history and the use of the historical method. The problems approach in general provides the opportunity for development of basic research skills: reading quickly for broad understandings and attentively for detail, taking useful and reliable notes, distinguishing between primary and secondary sources, evaluating evidence, and organizing and synthesizing data.

The interpretations approach adds to these the means of making the student familiar with the range and variety not only of the sources of history, but also of historical interpretation. Moreover, because of this special orientation, it demands both wider and more discriminating reading than does a standard problems course. Its peculiar character invests it with greater need for critical thinking because in operation it resolves upon the juxtaposition of at least two conflicting opinions. Moreover, its essential character invests it with greater need for critical thinking, in that, beyond the historical focus of a standard problems approach, the interpretations approach advances concern for thought about history. In its capacity for development of skills in critical thinking and reading in depth, the interpretations approach is unsurpassed. The final phase of investigation, as described in Chapter II, suggests a program of reading that carries beyond the requirements of the conventional course; although the survey approach does offer opportunity for wide lateral reading, it does not, of its nature, require reading in depth.

The preparation of a written report—a "position paper"—for each topic requires attention to logical organization and precision in writing, thus necessitating the development of those sophisticated writing skills so often neglected in high school courses.

THE ESSENCE OF HISTORY

In terms of the letter and spirit of scholarship, the conventional presentation of American history in chronological survey form carries with it two inherent and basic weaknesses: first, it lacks an intrinsic power of motivation which the interpretations approach provides in both organization and controversial content; second, it lacks the depth or the third dimension that derives from the application of interpretations of history. When the purpose of teaching American history is defined in terms of the development of understandings and critical thinking, the interpretations approach demonstrates the greatest capacity for satisfying those purposes.

NEEDS OF SOCIETY

The second of the considerations governing instruction in the "social studies" advanced by Professor Beard in the *Charter for the Social Sciences in the Schools* is that of "the realities and ideas of the society in which (social studies teaching) is carried on." It is in connection with this consideration that the possibility of reasonable, objective analysis of the purposes of teaching history (or the social studies) comes to a halt amid obscurities, shifting definitions, statements of literally hundreds of objectives reflecting the personal interest of reformers and committees, and open conflict between partisans of separate academic disciplines.

ROMANTIC UNREALITY

Almost every conceivable purpose that could be claimed for instruction in any field is to be found among the objectives listed for the social studies. The statements fail utterly to recognize the differentiated purposes of the various disciplines within the social studies as a whole as contrasted with those of other fields. The multiplicity and diffuseness of the statements of objectives are matched by their vagueness, inconsistency, and romantic unreality. An unfortunate teacher who attempted to follow such lists would rival Stephen Leacock's hero, who mounted his horse and rode off in all directions. Slogans and stereotypes abound, and there is little evidence that the implications for instruction are understood. Indeed, the listing of objectives seems to be a formality that must be attended to as a matter of ritual rather than the setting up of clear purposes and points of view by which instruction is to be shaped and appraised.[13]

The fundamental purpose of the teaching of the social sciences as stated in the *Charter* was the creation of "rich, many-sided personalities, equipped with practical knowledge and inspired by ideals. . . ." The *Charter* mentions the importance of information, though without defining what or how much; of skills, "not limited to academic operations," but as "the secrets of achievement in vocations, in personal affairs, in social situations." Further, it noted the aim of developing good habits—

7

personal cleanliness, industry, courtesy, promptness, accuracy, and effective co-operation; and of promoting attitudes such as respect for the rights and opinions of others, zeal for truth, pride in achievement, admiration, faith, loyalty, sense of responsibility, and desire to participate. All eminently admirable aims, but few, other than those heretofore considered, fall within the exclusive province of social studies, to say nothing of the even narrower range of the study of history, and, most important, few can be translated into course outlines.

Professor Jacques Barzun later provided a pointed review indicating more specific applications of the effort to bring the curriculum into line with social romanticism:

> Recall the furor over American history. Under new and better management that subject was to produce patriots—nothing less. An influential critic, head of a large university, wants education to generate a classless society; another asks that education root out racial intolerance (in the third or the ninth grade, I wonder?); still another requires that college courses be designed to improve labor relations. One man, otherwise sane, thinks the solution of the housing problem has bogged down—in the schools; and another proposes to make the future householders happy married couples through the schools. Off to one side, a well-known company of scholars have got hold of the method of truth and wish to dispense it as a crisis reducer. Adopt our nationally advertised brand and avert chaos.
>
> . . . Above and beyond all these stand the unabashed peacemakers who want Kitty Smith from Indiana to be sent to Germany, armed with Muzzey's *American History,* to undo Hitler's work.[14]

The numberless committee reports which define the needs, propose the objectives, prescribe the necessary curriculum changes, suggest the superior methods, and describe the optimum conditions under which the needs of society are best served, receive little attention from Kitty Smith, American history teacher in Indiana who, along with her colleagues on the actual firing line, would also agree with the Columbia Dean that "Free compulsory 'education' is a good thing, an indispensable thing, but it will not make the City of God out of Public School No. 26."

CITIZENSHIP: MORE ROMANTIC UNREALITY

At the peak of the Progressive era, the U.S. Bureau of Education published the 1916 *Report of the Committee on the Social Studies,* comprising seven specific recommendations, of which six advanced the idea that the teaching of social studies should have as its primary purpose the defining of the individual's importance in terms of his society.

8

By treating history as part of a group of subjects, known collectively as "the social studies," and furthermore by dropping specific areas of historical study such as ancient history and American colonial history from the curriculum, it was hoped that the more important study of "citizenship" might be stressed.

The cultivation of good citizenship, however, is not the responsibility of the study of history, nor of any of the separate and distinct social sciences, nor is it the exclusive concern of any single department, nor even of the school, though all of these undoubtedly make their own contribution to the development of the individual character.

> Those who teach and write in the domain of social science in universities and colleges, even when they disclaim all didactic motives, consciously or unconsciously, aid in determining the forms and subject matter of instruction in the schools, by their choice of materials, their elimination and their emphasis. At all events, what they teach and write has an effect on students who come within the range of their influence; by accident or design, it helps to set the pattern of civic training in the lower ranges. Although their intent may be formless and shadowy, it has an outcome.[15]

The formless influence is present throughout the elementary and high school years, without benefit of formal mention in any course outline or statement of purposes; present too in what Professor Beard styled "the laboratory of life," continually defining and redefining the character of the individual's citizenship. By clearing the high school curriculum of more narrowly conceived subject matter in favor of those courses more attuned to the conceived aims of society, the 1916 *Report of the Committee on the Social Studies* places emphasis upon training for effective citizenship and upon the inculcation of good habits, attitudes, and behavior. All serve to underscore the wisdom underlying Charles Beard's distinction between realities and social ideas.

ATTITUDES: STILL MORE ROMANTIC UNREALITY

The twenty-one members who made up the committee wisely recognized that if history were to be made "functional," so that it could be shaped to serve the desired, predetermined objective—the cultivation of good citizenship—then its essential character would have to be changed since the nature of the study of history did not easily adapt itself to producing desired results. The lot of the propagandist is a much happier one than that of the historian and teacher whose studies may well prove inconclusive or even embarrassing, and who, finding not infrequently that the walls of his pet argument are but paper, is continually remined that he who rides tiger must go where tiger goes. As Professor

9

Beard points out, social science that is truly scientific is neutral. This is the attitude that characterizes all research worthy of the name, that the teacher must instill in his students as he initiates them in the study of history.

Among the incidental values that might logically proceed from the interpretations approach are development of a habit of accuracy, of attitudes of healthy skepticism in dealing with the spoken and printed word, and of toleration of differing opinions. Yet, the American history survey, Latin I, geometry, or home economics would serve the habit of accuracy as well; nor does the development of either attitude depend upon the study of history.

More important, the value of the study of history requires no justification other than that which proceeds quite naturally from itself. The value of the proposed interpretations approach lies in its capacity for satisfying four controlling purposes of American history teaching:

(1) to familiarize the student in depth with the subject matter of American history;
(2) to introduce him to the writings of men who have given great thought to American history;
(3) to encourage in him the maturer understandings of events in American history that make its study meaningful;
(4) to develop his skill in the use of the historical method.

These purposes are served as well by no other approach.

NOTES

[1] Charles A. Beard, *A Charter for the Social Studies in the Schools* (New York: Charles Scribner's Sons, 1932), p. 2.

[2] *The Study of History in Schools; Report of the Committee of Seven to the American Historical Association* (New York: Macmillan, 1899), p. 102 ff. "In our judgment, sources are not intended to be either the sole or the principal materials for school study." The members were Andrew C. McLaughlin, Chairman, Herbert B. Adams, George L. Fox, Albert B. Hart, Charles H. Haskins, Lucy M. Salmon, and H. Morse Stephens.

[3] *Theory and Practice in Historical Study: A Report of the Committee on Historiography* (New York: The Social Science Research Council, 1946).

[4] Gilbert Highet, *The Art of Teaching* (New York: Vintage Books, 1950), pp. 112–113.

[5] *Theory and Practice in Historical Study: A Report of the Committee on Historiography* (New York: The Social Science Research Council, 1946).

[6] Henry Johnson, *Teaching of History* (New York: Macmillan, rev. 1940). Note his chapters 1, 15, and 16 on historical method and its applications in

teaching. He recognizes also the need for information and the use of information to develop understandings.

[7] Michael Oakeshott, *Rationalism in Politics and Other Essays* (London: Methuen, 1962), p. 166.

[8] Henry Johnson, *op. cit.*, p. 121. See also Robert L. Schuyler, "Some Historical Idols," *Political Science Quarterly*, Vol. XLVII, No. 1, March, 1932. Also Charles M. McIlwain, No. 2, January, 1937: "As historians, our real task is with history, not with its application. . . ." (p. 223).

[9] Jacques Barzun, *The Teacher in America* (New York: Anchor Books, 1954), p. 100.

[10] William H. Cartwright and Richard L. Watson, Jr. (eds.), *Interpreting and Teaching American History*, Thirty-First Yearbook of the National Council for the Social Studies, 1961, p. 4, quoted from G. Stanley Hall (ed.), *Methods of Teaching History* (Ginn, Heath, 1835), p. 120.

[11] See *Teaching of History*, especially Chapter 15, "School History and the Historical Method."

[12] Erling M. Hunt and others, *High School Social Studies Perspectives* (Boston: Houghton Mifflin, 1962). See Chapter I, "Changing Perspectives in the Social Studies," by Erling M. Hunt.

[13] Ernest Horn, *Methods of Instruction in the Social Studies* (New York: Scribner's, 1937), pp. 3–4.

[14] Jacques Barzun, *op. cit.*, pp. 11–12.

[15] Charles Beard, *Charter*, p. 87.

Two: Unit Outlines in the Interpretations Approach to American History

Basically, the interpretations approach utilizes a problems organization aimed at depth rather than breadth, but not, however, to the exclusion of the latter. The present proposal comprises a carefully structured examination of nine central questions, posed in terms of probably the maximum number feasible, sharply conflicting interpretations that focus attention upon selected major developments in American history. The examination of each of the central questions proceeds through three distinct steps or phases.

The function of the first phase of inquiry is to introduce the problem in its most basic context. Was the American Revolution a struggle against tyranny or was it an unfortunate accident? The teacher presents both positions to the students through lectures, carefully selected excerpts from historical works that support each of the two positions, and through the assignment and class discussion of additional selected articles which pose the two alternatives. The initial inquiry is completed with the students' identification of the several crucial arguments that support the conclusions of each of the two positions. The need for teacher direction in this analysis and identification of major points should diminish as the students develop their skill in critical reading. With the aid of duplicated materials, the Phase One presentation of the problem should be accomplished within one week.

The second phase comprises teacher-directed library research in which students gather the information that will verify or refute the major premises of both cases. The teacher guides the student to further readings in both secondary and primary sources. Obviously, in the initial units particularly, careful construction of subordinate questions, selection of conflicting opinions, and identification of sources are essential to success. The second phase demands a more flexible time schedule, varying from two to three weeks.

The primary objective of the final phase is, through class discussion, to draw conclusions respecting the central and subordinate questions, and to present student syntheses and critiques. The teacher may find that this final phase, which is one of summary and collation, is also a suitable opportunity to introduce, by lecture or student reports, new material that relates both to the original central question and to newly-emerging subordinate questions, and that serves to fill in gaps and to suggest possible alternative solutions to the questions originally posed.

The question of introducing new materials during the final phase of examination of the problem lies entirely within the discretion of the individual teacher, who must take into account innumerable circumstances of his own situation—time, student interest and capacity, relevance, and other factors. It is expected that the relevance or pertinence of such new material will suggest itself during the course of personal examination of the central question, and in the light of the most up-to-date scholarship. By way of illustration, the outline herein provided will suggest from time to time what such relevant considerations might be. The conclusion thus provides perspective on what has been covered, and may, at the same time, suggest the possibilities remaining open to continued research and interpretation—and to demonstration of the nature of history. The concluding phase should take a week. Allowing four weeks per topic, the thirty-six to forty-week school year suggests a maximum of nine units. However, the variation in number, as well as the selection of central and subordinate questions, is primarily a matter of individual choice, and is conditioned by the time factor, differences in student ability, and variations in library and teacher resources. Nor is it necessary for the teacher to adopt the proposal in its entirety. Since variety in approach is also a key factor in maintaining student interest in most subject matter, a judicious mixture, the interpretations approach to some units and the more conventional approach to others appears practicable.

The purpose of the outlines that follow is to demonstrate the kind of questions involved in an interpretations approach, to suggest specific readings having application to these questions, and to indicate the more widely available, inexpensive collections of both secondary readings and primary source materials. The interpretations approach may proceed successfully, however, from a carefully structured analysis of only two well-chosen conflicting viewpoints.

The American Revolution

Struggle against Tyranny or Unfortunate Accident?

Attempts to explain why the Americans fought a war with Great Britain from 1775 to 1783 divide generally into two broad and conflicting groups. Historians in one group advance the view that the war was a struggle of Americans against intolerable political and economic oppression by England. They underscore the difference existing between Americans and British that stirred the colonists to revolt. The second group maintains that the British colonial system was not oppressive and that the differences between the mother country and her colonies were not in fact as great as the natural bonds that tied them together. They assert that the rebellion was indeed unnecessary.

Was the American Revolution a struggle against tyranny or an unfortunate accident?

A. General statements on the causes of the American Revolution. Read one of the following.*

Wesley Frank Craven, "The Revolutionary Era," in John Higham (ed.), *The Reconstruction of American History,* 46–63.

Edmund S. Morgan, *The American Revolution: A Review of Changing Interpretations,* Service Center for Teachers of History, American Historical Association.

Page Smith, "David Ramsay and the Causes of the American Revolution," in John C. Wahlke (ed.), *The Causes of the American Revolution,* Problems in American Civilization Series, 113–123.

B. Specific interpretations of the causes. Read both of the following.

Lawrence Henry Gipson, "The American Revolution as an Aftermath of the Great War for the Empire, 1754–1763," reprinted in: Abraham

* Titles given below, with their publishers, are marked with an asterisk (*) in Appendix A.

S. Eisenstadt (ed.), *American History: Recent Interpretations*, I, 157–172; Sidney Fine and Gerald S. Brown (eds.), *The American Past: Conflicting Interpretations of the Great Issues*, I, 62–76; Wahlke (ed.), 37–49.

Edmund S. Morgan, "The American Revolution: Revisions in Need of Revising," in Eisenstadt, I, 173–185; Fine and Brown, I, 77–87.

C. Issues that underlie the conflicting interpretations. Using recommended sources, investigate one subsection (1a, 1b, 2a, 2b, 2c, 3a, 3b) of main questions 1, 2, and 3. Present a position paper logically organized and clearly and correctly written. Be concise and support your conclusions with specific evidence. Note your authority. Please note, as they occur, the excerpts illustrating the conflicting interpretations, from works to be read in their entirety.

1. Were British colonial economic policies just?

To begin with, we note that the thirteen colonies experienced a phenomenal development during the 150 years in which they were subject to the regulating policies of English mercantilism. . . . After 1763 the story is different. . . . In its total effect, British policy as it affected the colonies after 1763 was restrictive, injurious, negative. . . . Curtis P. Nettels, in Eistenstadt, I, 146.

. . . the mounting Anglo-French rivalry in North America from 1750 onward, the outbreak of hostilities in 1754, and the subsequent nine years of fighting destroyed the old equilibrium. . . . Attempts on the part of the Crown and Parliament to restore . . . the old balance led directly to the American constitutional crisis, out of which came the Revolutionary War and the establishment of American Independence. Lawrence Henry Gipson, in Eisenstadt, I, 172.

a. Did the British mercantile system operate to mutual advantage? in theory? in fact? in commerce? in both British and American manufactures? Were British land and currency policies just? Did mercantilism allow for economic differences within the colonies?

Charles M. Andrews, "A Note on the Economic Interpretation," in Wahlke, 13–21.

Oliver M. Dickerson, "Were the Navigation Acts Oppressive?" in Wahlke, 22–36.

Curtis P. Nettels, "British Mercantilism and the Economic Development of the Thirteen Colonies," in Eisenstadt, I, 137–147.

Louis B. Wright, "Imperial Prosperity from Southern Plantations," in Eisenstadt, I, 53–64.

b. Did Parliament levy unjust taxes upon the colonies? In the Grenville Program? Townshend Acts? Tea Tax? Declaratory Act?

Bernhard Knollenberg, "British Provocations in the Movement for Independence," in Wahlke, 50–53.

2. Were the political principles of Britain and of her colonies irreconcilably different?

This democratic ideal burst forth in England with some force in the sixteenth century and was reemphasized at a time and under conditions which permitted experiment in the America just discovered. The active, inquiring scholars from East Anglia . . . represented an attitude which was to become more frequently discernible in England . . . and to which American democracy was to owe much of its essential quality. Roy F. Nichols, in Eisenstadt, I, 35.

If the British government could not run the empire without bringing on evils that appeared insufferable to men like Washington, Jefferson, John Adams, and Franklin, then the burden of proof would seem to be on those who maintain that it was fit to run an empire. Edmund S. Morgan, in Eisenstadt, I, 178.

a. Did British practices infringe upon colonists' "Rights of Englishmen"?

b. Did the colonists fulfill the duties of Englishmen in their financial and military support of the war with France? in the Quartering Act? in the Intolerable Acts? in the Supremacy of Parliament? in the Writs of Assistance?

James T. Adams, "The Role of Merchants and Radicals," in Wahlke, 104–112.

c. Was a revolutionary democratic tradition developing in the colonies that was no longer compatible with English political ideas?

Carl Becker, "The Spirit of '76," in Wahlke, 86–103.

Merrill Jensen, "Democracy and the American Revolution," in Wahlke, 71–85.

Richard B. Morris, "Benjamin Franklin's Grand Design," in Eisenstadt, 147–157.

Roy F. Nichols, "English Origins of American Politics," in Eisenstadt, 32–52.

Clinton Rossiter, "The American Consensus," in Wahlke, 54–70.

3. Was the American Revolution a civil war between Haves and Have-nots?

The stream of revolution, once started, could not be confined within narrow banks, but spread abroad upon the land. Many economic desires, many social aspirations were set free by the political struggle, many aspects of colonial society profoundly altered by the forces thus let loose. The relations of social classes to each other, the institution of slavery, the system of land-holding, the course of business, the forms and spirit of the intellectual and religious life, all felt the transforming hand of revolution, all emerged from under it in shapes advanced many degrees nearer to those we know. J. Franklin Jameson, in *The American Revolution Considered as a Social Movement*, p. 11.

". . . as historians we should stop projecting into the eighteenth century the particular economic and social antagonisms that we have found in later generations. We may still believe that the American Revolution was in part a contest about who should rule at home, but we should beware of assuming that people took sides in that contest according to whether or not they owned property. And we should totally abandon the assumption that those who showed the greatest concern for property rights were not devoted to human rights." Edmund S. Morgan, in Eisenstadt, I, 182–183.

a. Did any particular social classes or religious sects collectively support or oppose the Revolution? If so, what were their motives?

Louis Hacker, "Economic and Social Origins of the American Revolution," in Wahlke, 1–17.

Frederick B. Tolles, "The American Revolution Considered as a Social Movement: a Re-evaluation," in Fine and Brown, I, 122–133.

Clarence L. Ver Steeg, "The American Revolution Considered as an Economic Movement," in Fine and Brown, I, 133–142.

17

b. Did any geographic section collectively support or oppose the Revolution? If so, what were its motives?

D. Conclusion. Why do historians differ? Which of the two interpretations is more nearly right?

1. What did leaders in Great Britain and in the American colonies say at the time?

2. Can both interpretations be right?

E. Related questions for investigation.

1. Were all leaders in Great Britain united against the colonies?

2. Were all Americans united against the British Government?

3. Was propaganda a factor in causing the Revolution?

4. Was the American Revolution a civil war? a world war?

5. What influence did the American Revolution have upon Great Britain? on France? on Canada? on Latin America?

The Constitution

Rejection or Reaffirmation of the Declaration of Independence?

Richard B. Morris suggests that the varying interpreters of the nature and origins of the United States Constitution can be distinguished as belonging to two camps. Historians of the so-called Anti-Federalist camp argue that the Constitution was the creation of a small group of determined men seeking only their personal economic security through the establishment of a strong central government which they themselves intended to control. In effect, these historians contend, the Constitution was a rejection of the principles of the Declaration of Independence; it was a counter-revolution, a reactionary instrument designed to serve the rich at the expense of the masses. Its authors made only those reluctant concessions of rights necessary to coax their liberal opponents to accept the new government.

Historians of the so-called Federalist camp view the document as a reaffirmation of the principles expressed in the earlier Declaration of Independence. They argue that the struggle for the ratification of the new Constitution was not as intense as has been suggested, and that most Americans recognized the need for a stronger government to protect the individual liberties won for them by the Revolution. Moreover, they contend that opposition to ratification of the Constitution was sporadic, unorganized, and in fact, non-existent in most states.

Was the Constitution a rejection or reaffirmation of the Declaration of Independence?

A. General statements on the nature of the Declaration of Independence, and of the Constitution of the United States. Read all of the following.*

* Titles given below, with their publishers, are marked with an asterisk (*) in Appendix A.

Carl Becker, "The Spirit of '76," in Wahlke, *Causes of the American Revolution,* Problems in American Civilization Series, 86–103.

Carl Becker, "What Is Still Living in the Political Philosophy of Thomas Jefferson," in Fine and Brown, I, 93–107.

Ralph Barton Perry, "The Declaration of Independence," in Earl Latham (ed.), *The Declaration of Independence and the Constitution,* Problems in American Civilization Series, 79–86.

Vernon L. Parrington, "The Great Debate," in Latham, 35–43.

B. Specific interpretations of the nature of the Constitution. Read Beard or Smith and at least one other.

Charles A. Beard, "An Economic Interpretation of the Constitution," in Fine and Brown, I, 179–195.

J. Allen Smith, "The Constitution as Counter-Revolution," in Latham, 30–34.

Douglass Adair, "The Tenth Federalist Revisited," in Fine and Brown, I, 195–213.

Henry Steele Commager, "The Constitution: Was It an Economic Document?" in Eisenstadt, I, 201–214.

Edward S. Corwin, "An Answer to the Economic Interpretation," in Latham, 62–65.

C. Issues that underlie the conflicting interpretations. Using recommended sources, investigate one subsection (1a, 1b, 2a, 2b, 2c) of main questions 1 and 2. Present a position paper logically organized and clearly and correctly written. Be concise and support your conclusions with specific evidence. Note your authority. Please note, as they occur, the excerpts illustrating the conflicting interpretations, from works to be read in their entirety.

1. Was the Constitution drafted by the rich for the benefit of the rich?

Of course, it may be shown . . . that the farmers and debtors who opposed the Constitution were, in fact, benefited by the general improvement which resulted from its adoption. . . . The point is, that the direct, impelling motive . . . was the economic advantages which the beneficiaries expected would accrue to themselves first, from their action. Further than this, economic interpretation cannot go. Charles A. Beard, in Fine and Brown, I, 195.

a. Did political instability under the Articles of Confederation pose a threat to property owners?

Merrill Jensen, "The Confederation Period: Perspectives and Significance," in Fine and Brown, I, 147–158.

Richard B. Morris, "The Confederation Period and the American Historian," in Fine and Brown, I, 147–158.

b. What were the political views of the delegates to the Constitutional Convention? What were their instructions?

Charles A. Beard, "An Economic Interpretation of the Contstitution," in Latham, 45–61. A view of the delegates themselves—material differing from that presented under the same title in Fine and Brown.

2. Was the Constitution the work of political idealists who hoped to destroy arbitrary government and affirm the principles of the Revolution?

In the process of studying Madison's ideas it will become apparent that it is highly anachronistic to tag his theory "anti-democratic" in the nineteenth- or twentieth-century meaning of the term. Madison's *Tenth Federalist* is eighteenth-century political theory directed to an eighteenth-century problem; and it is one of the great creative achievements of that intellectual movement that later ages have christened "Jeffersonian democracy." Douglass Adair, in Fine and Brown, I, 212–213.

a. How does eighteenth-century liberalism differ from twentieth-century liberalism? Similarly, how has the definition of conservatism changed? Does the text of the United States Constitution reflect eighteenth-century liberalism or conservatism?

How would you analyze the prescribed legislative process? the prescribed executive power? the prescribed judicial function? Was judicial review a Federalist or Republican device?

b. Why was the Bill of Rights omitted from the Constitution of 1787? Is the Constitution a flexible political device?

Alpheus T. Mason, "The Nature of Our Federal Union Reconsidered," in Eisenstadt, 214–226.

c. Did any particular group or class collectively support or oppose the ratification of the Constitution? What were their motives?

D. Conclusion. Why do historians differ? Which of the two positions has the better support?

E. Related questions for investigation.

1. What were the actual provisions of the Articles of Confederation concerning the power of the central government and its executive branch?

2. What is the significance of Shays Rebellion?

3. What were the proposals in the Constitutional Convention respecting the Executive Head?

4. Of what importance are the *Federalist Papers* to the interpreters of the period.

5. Who were the leaders in the Convention?

6. What were the views of the Constitution's opponents?

Jacksonian Democracy
Liberal Tradition or Conservative Reaction?

Historians' efforts to define the nature and significance of Jacksonianism have produced two conflicting views. Proponents of one view suggest that the tone of the movement, largely set by its leader, was unmistakably liberal. It was a continuation of the Jeffersonian agrarian democratic tradition which began in the first years of the nineteenth century, and which was characterized by sweeping social reform, extended suffrage, war on capitalist exploitation, help for the new working classes, and philosophical egalitarianism. A conflicting "Whig" interpretation asserts that the Jacksonian tradition was not liberal, but decidedly conservative; that Jackson was a strike-breaker, not the ally of labor; that he sought not to destroy exploitation, but to broaden its base; that he won elections, not as the champion of democracy and of extension of the franchise, but as the popular hero of New Orleans; and that the compelling drive of the Jacksonian democrat was not that of the dedicated egalitarian but that of the office seeker.

Was Jacksonian Democracy part of a liberal tradition in America or was it a conservative reaction?

A. General statements on the nature of Jacksonian Democracy. Read *one* of the following.*

* Titles given below, with their publishers, are marked with an asterisk (*) in Appendix A.

Charles Grier Sellers (ed.), *Jacksonian Democracy*, Service Center for Teachers of History, American Historical Association.

John William Ward, "The Age of the Common Man," in John Higham (ed.), *The Reconstruction of American History*, 82–97.

B. Issues that underlie identification of Jackson with a liberal tradition. Using recommended sources, investigate 1, 2, or 3. Present a position paper logically organized and clearly and correctly written. Be concise, and support your conclusions with specific evidence. Note your authority. Please note, as they occur, the excerpts illustrating the conflicting interpretations, from works to be read in their entirety.

1. Was Jackson a Jeffersonian Democrat? What were the basic characteristics of "Jeffersonian Democracy"?

There is, of course, no more obdurate problem in political philosophy than the problem of the one and the many, the difficulty being to reconcile the desirable liberties of the individual with the necessary powers of society; and Jefferson was no more successful in solving it than any other political philosophers have been.

. . . Jefferson agreed with Thomas Paine that whereas society is the result of our virtues government is the result of our vices and is therefore a necessary evil: necessary, in order to preserve order, protect property, and guarantee contracts; an evil, because inherently prone to magnify its authority and thereby impair the liberties of the individual. Carl Becker, in Fine and Brown, I, 99; reprinted from "What Is Still Living in the Political Philosophy of Thomas Jefferson," *American Historical Review,* XLVIII (July 1943).

Commerce was, to Jefferson, the great multiplier of national wealth and the disposer of agricultural surpluses.

. . . manufactures and crafts of the home and village seemed to him not only desirable, but also necessary to the ideal of a complete and interesting society . . . since (banking and finance) were the outworkings of, and bound up with, commerce and the maintenance of the public credit, he found it just as hard to get along without them as with them. . . . Joseph Dorfman, in Fine and Brown, I, 257.

The legendary Jefferson was an agrarian; and even as modern scholars were finding in his writings political precepts for an industrial age, the farmers of the United States were recognizing him as the founder of American agriculture and adopting him as their patron saint. Jefferson was not an agrarian fundamentalist; he did move with his times. No doubt the highly moral nature of his interest in public affairs and his pragmatic attitude would have led him, in the modern setting, to seek his end by modern means. Yet he started and ended life an agrarian at heart, and it was against an agrarian background that he saw his ideal of American democracy most clearly. So congenial was this background to him, and so vividly does it continue to display itself behind his legend, that it cannot be painted out of the portrait of Jefferson in modern dress. A. Whitney Griswold, in Fine and Brown, I, 271; reprinted from "The Agrarian Democracy of Thomas Jefferson," *American Political Science Review*, XL (August 1946).

2. How do Jacksonian and Jeffersonian ideas and practices differ with respect to: the place of the common man in politics? agrarian democracy? the spoils system? the working man? the nature and interpretation of the Constitution in theory and in practice? loose and strict construction? checks and balances? the courts? the limits and use of federal power? states' rights? the fostering of the American political party system? a national bank? internal improvements? the role of the federal government in labor and unions?

Ralph C. H. Catterall, "The Charges against the Bank," in George Rogers Taylor (ed.), *Jackson Versus Biddle*, Problems in Amercan Civilization Series, 36–53.

Bray Hammond, "Jackson, Biddle, and the Bank of the United States," in Taylor, 54–71; "Jackson's Fight with the Money Power," in Eisenstadt, I, 291–301.

Arthur M. Schlesinger, Jr., "The Bank War," in Taylor, 72–112; "Hard Money," in Fine and Brown, I, 399–414.

3. To what extent can differences between Jacksonianism and the Jeffersonian tradition be traced to physical changes wrought in America between 1800 and the 1830's?

C. Conclusion. Why do historians differ? Are the differences here based on more subjective judgments than those in Topics I and II?

D. Related questions for investigation.

1. What was Jackson's view of the presidency and of strong presidents?

2. What were Jackson's views on political parties?

3. What was the situation of labor organizations in Jackson's time?

5. What was the United States policy toward the Indians?

6. Was Jackson or Jefferson more inclined toward the use of a "Spoils System"?

7. Was Jackson's "Kitchen Cabinet" a liberal or a conservative influence?

8. Did Jackson advance or impede the changes in American life that were occurring during his presidency?

Westward Expansion

"Manifest Destiny" or Economic Imperialism?

The history of the United States and of the American people is a story of territorial expansion, extending across the continent from sea to sea, and beyond the water's edge to "contiguous" islands. The motives that prompted this drive for territorial acquisition have given rise to much historical speculation. Primarily, the attempt to identify the motives for American expansion have been concentrated in an investigation of the reasons why America undertook to fight three wars commonly considered to be wars of acquisition: the War of 1812, the Mexican War, and the Spanish-American War. In each instance historians have advanced either the conclusion that Americans were compelled primarily by their devotion to liberty and an attendant compulsion to spread it far and wide—an unmistakable missionary spirit that Albert K. Weinberg defines as "Manifest Destiny"—or the less idealistic conclusion that the primary compulsion can be reduced to the desire for material gain.

Clearly, evidence can be found to support either conclusion in all three instances, but can we identify one or the other as the compelling factor in the story of territorial expansion?

Was territorial expansion a result of "Manifest Destiny" or was it economic imperialism?

A. General statements on the nature of America's westward expansion. Read all of the following.*

* Titles given below, with their publishers, are marked with an asterisk (*) in Appendix A.

John A. Hobson, "Imperialism," in Theodore P. Greene (ed.), *American Imperialism in 1898*, Problems in American Civilization Series, 1–13.

William L. Langer, "A Critique of Imperialism," in Greene, 13–20.

Albert K. Weinberg, "Extension of the Area of Freedom," in Fine and Brown, I, 500–525.

B. Issues that underlie the nature of westward expansion. Using recommended sources, investigate one of main questions 1, 2, 3, or 4, or one subsection—5a, 5b, or 5c—of question 5. Present a position paper logically organized and clearly and correctly written. Be concise and support your conclusions with specific evidence. Note your authority. Please note, as they occur, the excerpts illustrating the conflicting interpretations, from works to be read in their entirety.

1. What is "Manifest Destiny"?

2. Was the War of 1812 an aspect of "Manifest Destiny" or a struggle for maritime rights?

If the real grievances which caused the war were interference by Great Britain with American commerce and the rights of American sailors, why was war to redress those grievances opposed by the maritime section of the nation and urged by the inland section, which they scarcely affected?

. . . without the peculiar grievances and ambitions of the West there would have been no war. Julius W. Pratt, in Fine and Brown, I, 296, 299.

On June 26, Monroe wrote to Russell informing him of the declaration of war and at the same time authorizing him to arrange an armistice immediately, "if the orders-in-council are repealed, and no illegal blockades are substituted for them, and orders are given to discontinue the impressment of seamen from our vessels, and to restore those already impressed.". . . The impressment issue was the rock that wrecked the last hope of peace. Alfred L. Burt, in Fine and Brown, I, 308, 309.

Reginald Horsman, "Western War Aims, 1811–1812," in Eisenstadt, I, 252–267.

3. Did the United States provoke war with Mexico in 1846? Who opposed the war with Mexico? Why? Who supported the war with Mexico? Why?

Bernard DeVoto, "Build Thee More Stately Mansions," in Fine and Brown, I, 476–500.

4. Was the Spanish-American War a reflection of the traditional American "Manifest Destiny" spirit?

Thus . . . duty and interest alike, duty of the highest kind and interest of the highest and best kind, impose upon us the retention of the Philippines, the development of the islands, and the expansion of our Eastern commerce. Henry Cabot Lodge, in Greene, 76.

Julius Pratt, "Manifest Destiny and the American Century," in Eisenstadt, 46–55.

Before the war there had not been the slightest demand for the acquisition of the Philippine Islands. The average American citizens could not have told you whether Filipinos were Far Eastern aborigines or a species of tropical nuts.

. . . President McKinley himself had to look them up on the globe; he could not have told their locality, he said, within two thousand miles. Samuel F. Bemis, in Greene, 88.

5. Or was the Spanish-American War fought on behalf of special interests?

5a. On behalf of business interests?

. . . the financial and business interests of the country were opposed to the war. James Ford Rhodes, quoted in Greene, 27.

On the other hand, Professor H. U. Faulkner, in his excellent *American Economic History,* contends that the expansion of American industrial and financial power had created a readiness for "financial imperialism," which "provided the great cause for the war." Julius W. Pratt, in Greene, 27.

5b. On behalf of trade?

American trade in the Orient had been an object of solicitude on the part of the Government from the foundation of the Republic. Charles A. Beard, in Greene, 24.

Julius W. Pratt, "The Large Policy of 1898," in Fine and Brown, II, 198–217.

5c. Or was the war a result of propaganda?

In the opinion of the writer, the Spanish-American War would not have occurred had not the appearance of Hearst in New York journalism precipitated a bitter battle for newspaper circulation. Joseph E. Wisan, in Greene, 52.

Richard Hofstadter, "Manifest Destiny and the Philippines," in Greene, 54–70.

George W. Auxier, "The Propaganda Activities of the Cuban *Junta* in Precipitating the Spanish-American War, 1895–1898," in Fine and Brown, II, 217–232.

C. Conclusion. Why do historians differ?

D. Related questions for investigation.

1. Does "the West" mean the same in American History as "the Frontier"?

2. What is the process by which new states are added to the Federal Union?

3. How efficient was the United States Navy in the War of 1812? in 1898?

4. How efficient was the United States Army in the Mexican War? in 1898?

The Civil War

Avoidable or Irrepressible Conflict?

In the 1930's and 1940's a school of "revisionist" historians advanced a new dimension in the historiography of the Civil War. Earlier historians had differed in defining the fundamental cause of the conflict. Some suggested that the moral urgency to abolish slavery precipitated the final clash; others viewed the war as a states' rights struggle against centralized government; a third group claimed it to be a struggle for Southern independence. Charles Beard had posed the idea that the real contest was between industrial and agrarian interests for economic supremacy.

All views assumed the inevitability of the "irrepressible" conflict. The revisionists attacked this broad underlying assumption, developing the thesis of the "needless" war and describing instead a conflict that was indeed repressible. The basic premise of the revisionists was that none of the explanations advanced earlier, nor any combination of them, would serve as an adequate explanation for the final conflict.

Was the Civil War an avoidable or an irrepressible conflict?

A. General statements on the causes of the Civil War. Read one of the following.*

* Titles given below, with their publishers, are marked with an asterisk (*) in Appendix A.

Hal Bridges, *Civil War and Reconstruction,* Service Center for Teachers of History, American Historical Association, 1–12.

Don E. Fehrenbacher, "Disunion and Reunion," in Higham, *The Reconstruction of American History,* 98–118.

Thomas J. Pressly, "The Confusion of Voices," in Edwin C. Rozwenc (ed.), *The Causes of the American Civil War,* Problems in American Civilization Series, 217–225.

B. Specific conflicting interpretations of the causes. Read both the Randall and the Geyl essays in their entirety.

It was small minorities that caused the war; then the regions and sections got into it. No one seems to have thought of letting the minorities fight it out. Yet writers who descant upon the causation of the war write grandly of vast sections, as if the fact of a section being dragged into the slaughter was the same as the interests of that section being consciously operative in its causation. Here lies one of the chief fallacies of them all.

If one word or phrase were selected to account for the war, that word would not be slavery, or states rights, or diverse civilizations. It would have to be such a word as fanaticism (on both sides), or misunderstanding, or perhaps politics. James G. Randall, in Fine and Brown, 579, 580; also in Rozwenc, 169, 170; reprinted from "The Blundering Generation," *Mississippi Valley Historical Review,* XXVII (June 1940).

Allan Nevins, "The Needless Conflict," in Eisenstadt, I, 453–465.

And who will deny that sentiment, passion, extra-rational conviction, supply a fertile soil to the monster growths of misunderstanding and exaggeration, misrepresentation, hatred and recklessness! The question remains whether one is justified in labelling these extra-rational factors with contemptuous terms and deny to them, as Randall does, a rightful role in the drama of history, relegating them without further ado to the category of "artificial agitation," which can on no condition be reckoned among "fundamental causes." Pieter Geyl, in Fine and Brown, I, 597; also in Rozwenc, *Causes of the Civil War,* 195.

C. Issues underlying interpretations of the causes of the Civil War.
Using recommended sources, investigate one of questions 1, 2, 3, 4, 5, or 6.* Present a position paper logically organized and clearly

*Adapted from Kenneth Stampp (ed.), *The Causes of the Civil War,* © 1965. By permission of Prentice-Hall, Inc., Englewood Cliffs, New Jersey.

and correctly written. Be concise and support your conclusions with specific evidence. Note your authority. Please note, as they occur, the excerpts illustrating the conflicting interpretations, from works to be read in their entirety.

1. Was the Civil War brought about by the moral urgency of the slavery question?

Bernard DeVoto, "Slavery and the Civil War," in Edwin C. Rozwenc (ed.), *Slavery as a Cause of the Civil War,* Problems in American Civilization Series, 98–102.

Philip S. Foner, "Business and Slavery," in Rozwenc, *Slavery As a Cause of the Civil War,* 65–68.

John Hope Franklin, "Slavery and the Martial South," in Eisenstadt, I, 415–426.

Allan Nevins, "The Ordeal of the Union," in Rozwenc, *The Causes of the American Civil War,* Problems in American Civilization Series, 200–217.

Ulrich B. Phillips, "The Central Theme of Southern History," in Rozwenc, *Slavery as a Cause of the Civil War,* 17–21.

Ulrich B. Phillips, "Plantation Labor," in Fine and Brown, I, 370–383.

Charles W. Ramsdell, "The Natural Limits of Slavery Expansion," in Rozwenc, *Causes of the American Civil War,* 150–162.

James Ford Rhodes, "Slavery as a Single Cause," in Rozwenc, *Causes of the American Civil War,* 84–97.

Arthur M. Schlesinger, Jr., "A Note on Historical Sentimentalism," in Rozwenc, *Causes of the American Civil War,* 181–190.

Kenneth M. Stampp, "The Historian and Southern Negro Slavery," in Fine and Brown, I, 383–394.

2. Was the Civil War caused by either "Slave Power" or "Black Republican" conspiracies?

James Buchanan, "Republican Fanaticism as a Cause of the Civil War," in Rozwenc, *Causes of the Civil War,* 61–67.

Arthur C. Cole, "Lincoln's Election an Immediate Menace to Slavery in the States?" in Fine and Brown, I, 531–556.

J. G. de Roulhac Hamilton, "Lincoln's Election an Immediate Menace to Slavery in the States?" in Fine and Brown, I, 556–566.

Russell B. Nye, "The Slave Power Conspiracy: 1830–1860," in Rozwenc, *Slavery as a Cause of the Civil War,* 28–36.

Henry Wilson, "The Slave Power Conspiracy," in Rozwenc, *Causes of the American Civil War,* 70–76.

3. Did the South secede to prevent the subversion of states' rights?

Avery Craven, "The Breakdown of the Democratic Process," in Rozwenc, *Causes of the American Civil War,* 171–181.

Rollins G. Osterweis, "The Idea of Southern Nationalism," in Rozwenc, *Causes of the American Civil War,* 134–149.

Alexander H. Stephens, "The War for States Rights," in Rozwenc, *Causes of the American Civil War,* 67–69.

Charles S. Sydnor, "The Southerner and the Laws," in Eisenstadt, I, 401–415.

4. Did the North wage war in order to save popular government?

Alpheus T. Mason, "The Nature of Our Federal Union Reconsidered," in Eisenstadt, I, 214–226.

Roy F. Nichols, "American Democracy and the Civil War," in Eisenstadt, I, 443–453.

5. Was the Civil War the result of economic sectionalism?

Charles A. Beard, "The Approach of the Second American Revolution," in Rozwenc, *Causes of the American Civil War,* 98–119.

Frank L. Owsley, "The Southern Defense of the Agrarian Ideal," in Rozwenc, *Causes of the American Civil War,* 119–133.

6. Was there an irreconcilable cultural contrast between North and South that precipitated war?

John W. Draper, "The Conflict Arises from Natural Causes," in Rozwenc, *Causes of the American Civil War,* 76–83.

D. Conclusion. Why do historians differ?

1. Do all historians who were Southerners agree?

2. Have any Negro historians written about the causes of the Civil War?

Reconstruction

Exploitation of the South or Genuine Reform?

The disagreement arising with respect to the nature of postwar reconstruction of the Southern states divides into two conflicting attempts at self-justification. The Southern view indicts the North for the imposition of its "brutal power against the prostrate South"; its political and economic exploitation of the South; and its determination to destroy the entire Southern social system in its effort to grant the Negro not only equality, but supremacy. Basically, then, the Southern view regards "Black Reconstruction" as a program of unbridled vengeance upon the South, designed primarily to punish the "traitors" and to insure the preeminence of the Republican Party for a long time to come. The Northern view ranges from a denial of these charges to the postulation of the idea that the Reconstruction program worked a positive good. Some historians argue that the corruption in the South was a national phenomenon, not one peculiar to Reconstruction, and that Reconstruction governments in the states were efficient and basically honest. They portray the Radical Republican, the Carpetbagger, and the scalawag as genuine liberals. William E. B. DuBois suggests that Reconstruction offered the nearest thing to progressive reform the South had ever seen.

Was Reconstruction exploitation of the South or genuine reform?

A. General statements on the nature of Reconstruction. Read Weisberger and one other.*

Hal Bridges, *Civil War and Reconstruction*, Service Center for Teachers of History, American Historical Association, 12–19.

Don E. Fehrenbacher, "Disunion and Reunion," in Higham, 114–118.

* Titles given below, with their publishers, are marked with an asterisk (*) in Appendix A.

Bernard A. Weisberger, "The Dark and Bloody Ground of Reconstruction Historiography," in Eisenstadt, I, 495–513; repeated as first essay in Eisenstadt, II, 3–21.

B. Specific interpretations of the nature of Reconstruction. Read either Coulter, Randall, or Wilson and either Degler or Simkins.

The minority report of a Congressional committee declared, "History, till now, gives no account of a conqueror so cruel as to place his vanquished foes under the domination of their former slaves. *That was reserved for the radical rulers of this great Republic.* . . .

A Northern newspaperman who came down to see this amazing spectacle declared it was "barbarism overwhelming civilization by physical force" and "a wonder and a shame to modern civilization." E. Merton Coulter, in Fine and Brown, II, 10, 11; also in Edwin C. Rozwenc (ed.), *Reconstruction in the South,* Problems in American Civilization Series, 97, 98.

James G. Randall, "Reconstruction Debacle," in Rozwenc, 11–16.

Woodrow Wilson, "The Reconstruction of the Southern States," in Rozwenc, 1–11.

There is a myth of Reconstruction history to which most Americans, Northerners and Southerners alike, give credence. In brief outline it goes something like this. In 1867, a vengeful Congress placed the southern states under a military despotism which supported by its bayonets an alien regime in each of the states, composed of white adventurers—the carpetbaggers and scalawags—and their ignorant Negro allies. For a decade thereafter, the story continues, these regimes looted the treasuries of the southern states, impoverished the region with high taxes, denied the southern white people any say in their own governance, and spread terror throughout the Southland. Not until the withdrawal of federal troops in 1877, it is said, did this nightmare end and decency in government return to the South. As in most myths, there is some truth in this one; but a balanced picture of Reconstruction is quite different. Carl N. Degler, in Fine and Brown, II, 24–25. Reprinted here, by permission, from *Out of Our Past,* Harper and Row, 1958.

Francis B. Simkins, "New Viewpoints of Southern Reconstruction," in Rozwenc, 84–91.

C. Underlying problems in discerning the nature of Reconstruction.
Using recommended sources, investigate one of questions 1, 2, or

3. Present a position paper logically organized and clearly and correctly written. Be concise and support your conclusions with specific evidence. Note your authority. Please note, as they occur, the excerpts illustrating the conflicting interpretations, from works to be read in their entirety.

1. What were the objectives of the Radical Republican Congress?

Can they be discerned through an analysis of the Reconstruction legislation? What were they? What were the social views of Lincoln, Johnson? of Stevens, Sumner? How did the Presidential Reconstruction Plan compare with that of Congress? What motives prompted the enactment of the Tenure of Office Act?

2. Were the Radical Republicans in control of the Reconstruction programs in the states?

Of what significance was Republican misjudgment of Johnson? Did the goals or ambitions of Negroes, carpetbaggers, and scalawags coincide with those of the Republicans in Washington? How effectively did "restorationists" block Radical control in the individual states?

Horace Mann Bond, "Social and Economic Forces in Alabama Reconstruction," in Rozwenc, 32–50.

W. E. B. DuBois, "The Black Proletariat in South Carolina," in Rozwenc, 62–83.

Walter L. Fleming, "Civil War and Reconstruction in Alabama Reconstruction," in Rozwenc, 24–32.

Roger W. Shugg, "Class and Race Strife in Louisiana," in Rozwenc, 16–24.

Vernon Lane Wharton, "The Negro in Mississippi Politics," in Rozwenc, 51–62.

3. Did the Radical Republicans fulfill their stated and covert objectives?

How successful was the effort to implant equalitarian ideals? What was the significance of the election of 1876 for the southern Negro? What evidence, tangible and intangible, remains today of reform and improvement wrought during the Reconstruction Era?

D. Conclusion. Why do historians differ?

1. Do all historians who were southerners agree?

2. Have any Negro historians written about Reconstruction?

E. Related questions for investigation.

Develop a question related to one of the following topics.

The impeachment and trial of Andrew Johnson

The Freedman's Bureau

Carpetbaggers

Military Rule in any one of the Southern states

The Election of 1876

The Ku Klux Klan

Colleges for Negroes: The Peabody Fund or the Slater Fund; the Peabody Normal College, Hampton Institute, or Talladega College; or Booker T. Washington

The "New South"

The Gilded Age, 1865–1899

Abandonment of Morality or Period of Adjustment?

Students of the Gilded Age are often confronted with what appears to be an insoluble problem. Is the over-all development of America between the Civil War and the turn of the nineteenth century to be remembered with pride or with shame? The spectacular rise to industrial power of the United States, its impressive economic growth, and increased national income and production are all a matter of record. Historians have differed as to whether the leaders identified with the statistics of success are to be considered "robber barons" or "entrepreneurial statesmen." Business practices of the era which attended this spectacular growth have been condemned, and both national and local politics have been viewed as hopelessly corrupt. The very force of the reform movements which arose during the closing decades of the nineteenth century suggests that they were replacing a moral void. Was there no evidence of continuing patriotism and personal responsibility in American life? Had morality been sacrificed in the drive for wealth, or had the social, economic, and political structure changed so much as to necessitate the substitution of more modern principles—principles which could be established at length only with great difficulty by a patient, fundamentally moral people?

Was the Gilded Age a period of abandoned morality or of gradual adjustment?

A. General statement on interpretations of the gilded age. Read Miller or an approved alternative of your own choice.*

William Miller, "The Realm of Wealth," in Higham, 137–156.

* Titles given below, with their publishers, are marked with an asterisk (*) in Appendix A.

B. Introductory readings to a study of the gilded age. Read all selections.

Hal Bridges, "The Robber Baron Concept in American History," in Eisenstadt, II, 57–68.

Ralph Henry Gabriel, "The Gospel of Wealth and the Gilded Age," in Gail Kennedy (ed.), *Democracy and the Gospel of Wealth,* Problems in American Civilization Series, 55–67.

The Right Reverend William Lawrence, "The Relation of Wealth to Morals," in Kennedy, 68–76.

C. Conflicting interpretations in three areas of investigation. Using recommended sources, investigate either the economic sphere, the political sphere, or the social sphere. Present a position paper logically organized and clearly and correctly written. Be concise and support your conclusions with specific evidence. Note your authority. Please note, as they occur, the excerpts illustrating the conflicting interpretations, from works to be read in their entirety.

1. The economic sphere.

. . . Not only did the champions of evolution maneuver the clergy into the position of opposing freedom of teaching and of scholarship, but they also destroyed the religious sanction for morals by justifying ruthless methods in business and politics. "The survival of the fittest" became the rationale of those who shed moral scruples, in the business field at least, in their climb to wealth and economic power.

. . . the frontier spirit moved east to coalesce with Social Darwinism and complete the rationale of a new school of business leadership. Chester

McArthur Destler, in Fine and Brown, II, 24–25; reprinted from *Out of Our Past,* Harper and Row, 1959.

Matthew Josephson, "The Robber Barons," in Earl Latham (ed.), *John D. Rockefeller: Robber Baron or Industrial Statesman?,* Problems in American Civilization Series, 34–48.

Henry Demarest Lloyd, "The Old Self-Interest," in Latham, 68–76.

Ida M. Tarbell, "The Standard Oil Company," in Latham, 7–33.

Thorstein Veblen, "The Captain of Industry," in Kennedy, 102–111.

A conflicting interpretation.

Thomas C. Cochran, "The Legend of the Robber Barons," in Fine and Brown, II, 59–71.

William Graham Sumner, "The Concentration of Wealth: Its Economic Justification," in Kennedy, 81–85.

Related topics.

Gerald N. Grob, "The Knights of Labor and the Trade Unions, 1878–1886," in Eisenstadt, II, 99–113.

Theodore Saloutos, "The Agricultural Problem and Nineteenth-Century Industrialism," in Eisenstadt, II, 113–137.

2. The political sphere.

The parties of the period after the post-Civil War were based on patronage, not principle; they divided over spoils, not issues. Although American political parties are never celebrated for having sharp differences of principle, the great age of the spoilsmen was notable for elevating crass hunger for office to the level of a common credo. . . . In 1879 young Woodrow Wilson expressed in eight words his disgust with the degradation of American politics: "No leaders, no principles; no principles, no parties." Richard F. Hofstadter, in Fine and Brown, II, 173.

The course of administrative history, after Grant, was one of recovery from the abuses of the Civil War and of the first twelve years thereafter. Hard battles were fought between Congress and the executive branch, between an older generation wedded to politics and a new generation emerging in an age of business, between reformers and skeptics. Although improvements were painfully slow, there was substantially no regression. . . . Leonard D. White, in Fine and Brown, II, 194.

The government-business relationship.

The question of government intervention in business is handled well in the following pairs of conflicting interpretations, selected from Colston E. Warne (ed.), *The Pullman Boycott of 1894*, Problems in American Civilization Series.

John P. Altgeld, "Federal Interference in the Chicago Strike," 41–52.

Grover Cleveland, "The Government in the Chicago Strike of 1894," 52–63.

Eugene V. Debs, "The Federal Government and the Chicago Strike," 63–74.

Henry James, "A Defense of Richard Olney," 75–81.

Gustavus Myers, "The Supreme Court Decision as Evidence of Class Bias," 81–83.

Charles Warren, "The Supreme Court Decision," 84–85.

3. The social sphere.

Beginning with the law of 1882, which established federal supervision of immigration and excluded certain groups unable to support themselves, the restriction movement blossomed into a formidable and even violent crusade in the late eighties and nineties. John Higham, in Eisenstadt, II, 170.

Competition was glorious. Just as survival was the result of strength, success was the reward of virtue. Sumner could find no patience for those who would lavish compensations upon the virtueless. Richard F. Hofstadter, in Eisenstadt, II, 202.

We have noted, then, that the bulk of American Protestantism achieved during this period a working ideological harmony with the modes of the modern industrialized civilization, the free-enterprise system, and the burgeoning imperialism. Sidney E. Mead, in Eisenstadt, II, 194.

Frank Luther Mott, "The Magazine Revolution and Popular Ideas in the Nineties," in Eisenstadt, I, 230–243.

There are those who maintain, with Van Wyck Brooks, that somewhere in the process of expansion the college lost its soul. If it did, it was in the attempt, so characteristically American, to build more stately mansions. George P. Schmidt, in Eisenstadt, I, 229.

The acquiescence of Northern liberalism in the Compromise of 1877 defined the beginning, but not the ultimate extent, of the liberal retreat on the race issue. C. Vann Woodward, in Eisenstadt, I, 153.

D. Conclusion. Why do historians differ?

E. Related questions for investigation. Develop a question related to one of the following topics.

Architecture of the Gilded Age

Humanitarian movements
The Social Gospel
The Tweed Ring
The Homestead Strike or the Pullman Strike
Populism
The party platforms of 1896
Public education
Status of women
Black Friday

The New Deal

Evolution or Revolution?

A basic process of historical study involves the identifying of the origin or sources from which a given event or movement springs. The effort to place the New Deal in an historical perspective has produced two sharply different points of view with regard to its ancestral roots. Gerald Johnson, Eric F. Goldman, Basil Rauch, and others have suggested that the New Deal was a revival of the Progressive reform movement of the early 1900's. Others of the liberal-tradition school link the New Deal with the nineteenth century Populists, and Arthur M. Schlesinger, Jr., sketches a more distant connection with the earlier Jacksonian reforms. A second school, of which Richard Hofstadter is a leading spokesman, denies the evolutionary view of the New Deal and asserts that it represented a radical departure from the American reform tradition and was a sharp break with the past. Some repudiate the idea of its domestic origins, and equate it rather with anti-liberal foreign ideas, treating it as thinly veiled socialism and a bureaucracy.

Was the New Deal a phase in the evolution of reform or a distinct revolution?

A. General statements interpreting the New Deal and the American reform tradition. Read Freidel and either Mann or Mowry.*

Frank Freidel, "The New Deal in Historical Perspective," in Eisenstadt, II, 351–366.

Arthur Mann, "The Progressive Tradition," in Higham, 157–179.

George E. Mowry, *The Progressive Movement, 1900–1920: Recent*

* Titles given below, with their publishers, are marked with an asterisk (*) in Appendix A.

Ideas and New Literature, Service Center for Teachers of History, American Historical Association.

B. Specific interpretations of the nature of the New Deal. Read Goldman or Schlesinger and either Hacker or Hofstadter.

Many of the bills (of the New Deal) whisked through Congress bespoke the central idea common to both principal reform traditions, the New Freedom and the New Nationalism——the belief that the best solution for economic and social ills was action by the federal government under strong executive leadership. Eric F. Goldman, in Fine and Brown, II, 412.

Arthur M. Schlesinger, Jr., "Sources of the New Deal," in Eisenstadt, II, 338–350, is also a good statement of the evolutionary interpretation of the New Deal.

Louis M. Hacker, "The Third American Revolution," in Edwin C. Rozwenc (ed.), *The New Deal: Revolution or Evolution?*, Problems in American Civilization Series, 1–19 (1959), is a lucid statement of extreme "revolutionary" interpretation.

Still, granting that absolute discontinuities do not occur in history, and viewing the history of the New Deal as a whole, what seems outstanding about it is the drastic new departure that it marks in the history of American reformism. The New Deal was different from anything that had yet happened in the United States: different because its central problem was unlike the problems of Progressivism; different in its ideas and its spirit and its techniques. Richard Hofstadter, in Fine and Brown, II, 431–432.

C. Issues that underlie the conflicting interpretations. Using recommended sources, investigate one of questions 1, 2, 3, or 4. Present a position paper logically organized and clearly and correctly written. Be concise and support your conclusions with specific evidence. Note your authority. Please note, as they occur, the excerpts illustrating the conflicting interpretations, from works to be read in their entirety.

1. The central problem was unlike the problems of Progressivism. Was it unlike those of Populism?

John Kenneth Galbraith, "The Days of Boom and Bust," in Eisenstadt, II, 311–322.

Washington Gladden, "The Embattled Farmers," in George F. Whicher (ed.), *William Jennings Bryan and the Campaign of 1896,* Problems in American Civilization Series, 9–14.

James Laughlin, "Causes of Agricultural Unrest," in Whicher, 15–24.

Theodore Saloutos, "The Agricultural Problem and Nineteenth-Century Industrialism," in Eisenstadt, II, 113–136.

2. The New Deal was different in its ideas. Did it differ from New Nationalism? from the New Freedom? from Populism? from Associational Activities of the 1920's? Did it differ in its relief legislation?

James A. Barnes, "Myths of the Bryan Campaign," in Eisenstadt, II, 21–46.

John M. Blum, "President, Congress and Control," in Fine and Brown, II, 251–274.

John M. Blum, "Uses of Power," in Eisenstadt, II, 253–267.

John D. Hicks, "The Persistence of Populism," in Fine and Brown, II, 132–142.

Arthur S. Link, "What Happened to the Progressive Movement in the 1920's?" in Eisenstadt, II, 293–311.

George E. Mowry, "The California Progressive and His Rationale: A Study in Middle Class Politics," in Eisenstadt, II, 244–253.

3. The New Deal was different in its spirit. Did it differ from Populism? from Progressivism? from experimentalism? Did it differ in its crusading? in being labor-tainted? in its reform program?

Victor Ferkiss, "Populist Influences on American Fascism," in Fine and Brown, II, 132–168.

Matthew Josephson, "The Politics of Reform," in Fine and Brown, II, 237–251.

4. The New Deal was different in its techniques. Did it differ from Populism? from Progressivism? from Muckraking? Did it differ in its war on the Courts? in its recovery program? in its farms, labor and money regulation? in its bureaucracy?

Richard M. Abrams, "Woodrow Wilson and the Southern Congressmen, 1913–1916," in Fine and Brown, II, 287–304.

Robert E. Cushman, "The Supreme Court and the Constitution," in Alfred H. Cope and Fred Krinsky (eds.), *Franklin D. Roosevelt and the Supreme Court,* Problems in American Civilization Series, 60–70.

Bernard DeVoto, "Desertion from the New Deal," in Cope and Krinsky, 35–37.

Max Lerner, "The Supreme Court and American Capitalism," in Cope and Krinsky, 39–59.

Charles Seymour, "Woodrow Wilson: A Political Balance Sheet," in Eisenstadt, II, 279–289.

Rexford G. Tugwell, "The Compromising Roosevelt," in Eisenstadt, II, 366–386.

D. Conclusion. Why do historians differ? Are any of the reasons new?

E. Related questions for investigation.

1. Was the power granted the president by the National Industrial Recovery Act warranted by the circumstances?

2. Are there precedents in American history for any of the "alphabet agencies," CCC, TVA, AAA or WPA?

3. Did Herbert Croly's *The Promise of American Life* provide the intellectual basis for the New Deal?

4. What was the program of the Liberty League?

American Foreign Policy

Isolation or Commitment?

An analysis of the intent and circumstances of each of several major foreign policy developments might yield an identification of basic premises which have guided the formulation of American foreign policy from its inception to the present day.

It is possible that such an analysis might produce evidence of patterns of thinking or, conceivably, of what might be styled a "conditioned reflex" to certain international stimuli. The validity of any generalizations thus derived is obviously increased proportionately with the number and strength of the individual cases from which they have been drawn. Clearly, more conclusive generalizations require a broader sampling than the five significant considerations that follow, but even these few do provide a firm framework within which to develop an over-all concept of what the American foreign policy has been, although that concept must be tested and re-tested.

It has been suggested that an American foreign policy as such does not exist; that in reality we are dealing with a series of not necessarily connected policies formulated within their own unique context of time, space, and situation. Interest in the individual case is in no way diminished by the fact that collectively they do not suggest a trend or pattern, and it is as difficult to demonstrate that they do, as to show that they do not.

Has traditional American foreign policy reflected isolation or commitment?

A. General statements on interpretations in American foreign policy. Read the first item and either of the other two.*

* Titles given below, with their publishers, are marked with an asterisk (*) in Appendix A.

Ernest R. May, *American Intervention: 1917 and 1941,* Service Center for Teachers of History, American Historical Association.

Ernest R. May, "Emergence to World Power," in John Higham (ed.), *The Reconstruction of American History,* 180–196.

Alexander DeConde, *New Interpretations in American Foreign Policy,* Service Center for Teachers of History, American Historical Association.

B. Issues underlying identification of a foreign policy tradition. Present one position paper on Problem 1 or 2 *and* another position paper on Problem 3, 4, or 5. Please note, as they occur, the excerpts illustrating the conflicting interpretations.

1. Did George Washington, in his Farewell Address, prescribe a policy of isolation for the United States?

2. Was the Monroe Doctrine a policy of isolation or of commitment?

Samuel Flagg Bemis, "The Monroe Doctrine: Background and Statement," in Fine and Brown, I, 335–366.

Samuel Flagg Bemis, "The Monroe Doctrine: Diplomatic Background, Pronouncement, and Effect, 1815–1826," in Eisenstadt, I, 268–291.

Theodore R. Schellenberg, "Jeffersonian Origins of the Monroe Doctrine," in Fine and Brown, I, 314–335.

3. Why did the United States enter World War I?

It was our unneutral financing of the Allies that led to the resumption of German submarine warfare, and it was the resumption of this warfare which furnished the "incident" that enabled the war party in this country to put us into the conflict. It is, thus, perfectly clear that economic and financial pressure was the crucial factor which led us into war in 1917. Harry Elmer Barnes, in Fine and Brown, II, 315.

The point is not, therefore, that public opinion *forced* Wilson to accept the decision for war, but that it facilitated doing what Wilson for other reasons now thought was necessary and right to do. . . .

All this is said without any intention of implying that Wilson ever wanted war. The agony of his soul was great as he moved through the dark valley of his doubts. He had no illusions about the merits of the conflict

49

into which he and his people were being drawn. He saw the risks of intervention, both to his own nation and to the world, with remarkable clarity. But he could devise no alternative; and he set aside his doubts in the hope that acting now as a belligerent, with all the power and idealism of the American people sustaining him, he could achieve objectives to justify the misery of mankind. Arthur S. Link, in Fine and Brown, II, 344; reprinted from *Wilson the Diplomatist*, Johns Hopkins Press, 1957.

4. Why did the United States Senate reject the Versailles Treaty?

There is evidence, however, to demonstrate that he (Henry Cabot Lodge) was out to kill the league under any circumstance, and that he considered the best way to accomplish this was through attaching reservations to the covenant. Lodge was a partisan Republican willing to sacrifice ideals or anything else to party loyalty. From 1893 to 1924, as a member of the Senate, he never departed from strict party regularity. In addition to party regularity, he hated Woodrow Wilson. Walter Johnson, in Fine and Brown, II, 352.

The vital role of the loyal Democrats must be re-emphasized. If all of them who professed to want the treaty and had voted "Yea," it would have passed with more than a dozen votes to spare. If the strait-jacket of party loyalty had not been involved, the necessary two-thirds could easily have been mustered. Thomas A. Bailey, in Fine and Brown, II, 361.

5. Why did the United States enter World War II? What was the role of Franklin Delano Roosevelt in America's entrance?

It would ordinarily be assumed that the President, after reading this intercepted Japanese message, would hurriedly call a conference of the more important Army and Navy officers to concert plans to meet the anticipated attack. The testimony of General Marshall and Admiral Stark would indicate that the Chief Executive took the ominous news so calmly that he made no effort to consult with them. Did he deliberately seek the Pearl Harbor attack in order to get America into the war? Charles C. Tansill, in Fine and Brown, II, 470.

Of all the accusations made, the one most shocking to me is that Roosevelt and his chief advisers deliberately left the Pacific Fleet and base at Pearl Harbor exposed as a lure to bring about a direct Japanese attack upon us. . . .

A variant of this accusation, which at least does not require such a willingness to believe the worst, might also be noted—that despite ample knowledge that Pearl Harbor was about to be attacked, the American Government purposefully left it exposed and allowed the event to happen. Herbert Feis, in Fine and Brown, II, 473; reprinted from "War Came at Pearl Harbor: Suspicions Considered," *The Yale Review,* XLV (March 1956).

Dexter Perkins, "Was Roosevelt Wrong?" in Eisenstadt, II, 391–403.

George M. Walter (ed.), *Pearl Harbor: Roosevelt and the Coming of the War,* Problems in American Civilization Series.

C. Conclusion. Why do historians differ?

D. Related questions for investigation. In terms of isolation and commitment how would the American position on the following be defined?

The issue of freedom of the seas in the War of 1812, in World War I

The Open Door policy

The role of Theodore Roosevelt in the Treaty of Portsmouth

The World Court

The North Atlantic Treaty Organization

The United Nations

Three: Source Materials for the Interpretations Approach

The *sine qua non* of the interpretations approach to American history is an adequate library collection. Moreover, many of the books must be available in sufficient quantity to permit their use as needed by numbers of students working on the same problem at the same time. The cost of providing high school libraries with such collections in respectable depth has been greatly reduced by the publication of an almost overwhelming amount of suitable material in paperbound editions.

THE PAPERBACK AS HIGH SCHOOL STUDY MATERIAL

The less expensive method of publication has been accompanied by a marked increase in the number and variety of edited collections of documents, readings, and interpretations, making the problems and interpretations approaches a great deal more feasible than they have been in the past. The prohibitive cost of the clothbound textbook is contributing to the increased popularity and use of paperbound materials—a point certainly not lost upon publishers.

Unfortunately, the obvious disadvantage of the paperbound book is most pronounced in high school use, where it has been necessary to replace it continually. However, restricting the use of paperbound material to the classroom or the library prolongs its service, reducing the need for frequent replacement. The hurried, hazardous trips to and from a steel locker take a greater toll on the life of a volume in high school service than does the intense study to which it is irregularly subjected! Rarely is any text retired as unusable because of students' underscorings of important passages or other such serious notations. Were it possible to restrict the locus of use of study materials, both cloth and paperbound, books could be made to last indefinitely. The paperback collection, safeguarded by a modicum of care, will provide practical and economical service at the high school level. Recent improvements in covers and bindings have greatly increased their durability. It should also be noted that the classroom teacher can be helpful in prolonging the circulating life of a book once he succeeds in promoting the value of the book to the student in terms of its content rather than in terms of its newness.

THE COLLECTION OF SOURCES

Obviously, even though students are buying paperbacks increasingly, no student can be expected to provide himself with personal copies of all of the readings required for the proposed course, nor can the school be expected to furnish them for students on an individual basis. As suggested above, most of the needed materials can be made available to all students through the establishment of a library reserved shelf, or a classroom library, comprising enough copies of a single title—twenty-five for a class of twenty-five students—to serve the entire course enrollment on a one-class-at-a-time basis. The reserved shelf in the library has the advantage over the creation of a classroom library in imposing no additional responsibility, clerical or otherwise, upon the classroom teacher, who will be the more accessible to students seeking to make use of their free time during the day.

Most of the source material used in the interpretations approach should be available to students on the library reserved shelf. Non-circulating works should include all assigned reading and whatever readings are necessary to classroom and library investigation—overviews, readings, interpretations, and documents. Within this framework of the kinds of materials that constitute the operational source collection, there is considerable latitude for expenditure. The collection that must serve as many as twenty-five students at one time should include four or five copies of at least three reliable two-volume college texts in American history. These twenty or thirty clothbound volumes represent a permanent investment and ordinarily need not be replaced until outdated. The need for good basic overviews suggests those of the caliber of Carman and Syrett, Morison and Commager, or John D. Hicks. There are, of course, others. A collective effort of six eminent historians, newly introduced in 1963 by Harcourt, Brace and World, *The National Experience,* is as serviceable a one-volume history as one can find. The variety of texts adds the advantage of different perspective and the course objectives dictate acquisition of the widest variety possible. Two copies of Richard B. Morris' *Encyclopedia of American History* should also be available for general reference.

In addition to the several general survey texts, the teacher will make use of specialized texts in conjunction with the specialized unit. A unit on foreign policy requires copies of Thomas A. Bailey's *Diplomatic*

History of the American People, Samuel F. Bemis' *Diplomatic History of the United States,* and Julius Pratt's *History of United States Foreign Policy.* Merle Curti's *Growth of American Thought* and Vernon L. Parrington's *Main Currents in American Thought* should be included in multiple copies by the teacher who involves his class in American intellectual history.

The collection of readings, interpretations, and documents admit a much greater range of possibilities both in content and in cost. Most emphatically, greater expenditure does not necessarily identify the superior course.

Because of their organization in pairs of conflicting interpretations of major topics, the Sidney Fine and Gerald S. Brown volumes, *The American Past,* are ideally suited to the initial phase of investigation, and a library reserve of one copy per class member would provide basic readings at a cost of about $150, with a life expectancy comparable to that of a clothbound text in ordinary use. Additional sources, such as Abraham S. Eisenstadt's *American History: Recent Interpretations,* provide depth in historiography and need be available in fewer numbers. A dozen would seem adequate for a class of twenty-five.

A very successful interpretations approach can be effected through an exclusive use of almost any one collection of viewpoints. Any such collection should be done well enough to yield concisely stated conflicting viewpoints on American history topics. Key titles of the Problems of American Civilization (Amherst) series are ideally suited to serve in this capacity. Independent of supplemenary interpretations, they generally offer the greatest advantage of any single work in terms of cost, and in the presentation of a variety of major viewpoints on a given topic.

General surveys of the interpretations of selected topics are necessary to the student's understanding of the position and significance of each differing opinion within the framework of historical interpretation. The surveys provided in the Service Center for Teachers of History series, as well as John Higham's *Reconstruction of American History,* are available at low enough cost to permit each student to have his own copy.

Library subscriptions to historical journals, in particular *The Mississippi Valley Historical Review, The American Historical Review, New England Quarterly, Journal of Southern History,* and *William and Mary Quarterly,* are valuable in providing reviews of recent interpretations and articles by authorities on select topics. Students should learn of the existence and value of such publications before they enter college.

Where necessity dictates and inexpensive duplicating processes are at hand, the resourceful and enterprising teacher can reproduce enough source materials for student analysis to constitute a sound interpretations approach. Lectures and student reports can also provide overviews of interpretations and summaries of readings.

Primary source materials, accounts, and documents, can be obtained at prices starting from fifty cents. A half dozen copies of Henry S. Commager's *Documents of American History* is an indispensable part of the reserved shelf collection. Many other inexpensive collections on selected topics, such as Richard B. Morris' *The American Revolution,* can be put into the hands of the individual student to excellent advantage.

The circulating part of the library collection should include those works, chiefly monographs and biographies, useful to the final related considerations for each topic. The teacher should provide students with a listing of those works available in the circulating library that are appropriate to each unit. Works available to students on the normal circulation basis will also serve the purpose of providing historical background against which the particular questions are set, as well as initiating students in the habit of leisure reading in the field of history—an aspect of their education that should not be overlooked. The American history course that does not introduce the student to the writings of Edward Channing, Francis Parkman, and Henry Adams can be counted a loss in what is perhaps one of its most important functions, that of developing a lasting interest in history.

The first step in the establishment of a resource collection in the high school library consists of a careful inventory of those materials already on hand, and of an evaluation of what is available in terms of the course objectives. Often the departmental or library budget will dictate a gradual filling of gaps on a strict priority basis. The slower, more deliberate acquisition of the desired works often produces the more effectual collection. This method is in marked contrast to those systems in which everything must be bought at once, without forethought, without due estimation of needs, and with considerable risk of duplication and waste. Often the motivation is only to anticipate the local Board's call for a progress report, or to avoid the lapse of an appropriation.

Nor is it necessary to launch the interpretations approach in its entirety, lacking either adequate source materials or teachers experienced in their use, or both. Increasing library resources and experience on a unit-by-unit basis is sound procedure. The interpretations approach can be inaugurated, for example, with a unit on the Causes of the Civil War, making exclusive use of twenty-five reserved copies of Kenneth Stampp's *Causes of the Civil War;* or perhaps on an individual ownership basis. It must be remembered, however, that classroom experimentation with one or two interpretations units within the conventional high school approach is likely to yield more definitive conclusions respecting the strength of the teacher and the library than the over-all value of an interpretations approach.

THE FUNCTION OF THE STUDENT'S TEXTBOOK

One of the more unfortunate characteristics of our high school system today has been the continuing emphasis upon the textbook in social studies classes. In many cases the text has displaced the teacher as the principal source of instruction. This substitution has been abetted by those approaches in which the teacher elicits a recitation of the reading assignment from unenthusiastic students, who must eventually conclude that American history is enclosed in its entirety between the covers of a single volume, written, more often than not, with something less than inspiration. The contribution of the teacher, who presumably has chosen the study of history or one of the social sciences as his life's interest, is drastically minimized. This form of instruction has engendered the misapprehension, of regettably wide currency, that anyone can teach history. Instances of non-social science majors being assigned to "teach" a course or two in the high school social studies program are not uncommon. The wider implications of such a confusion include the idea that social studies instruction is a dispensable part of the high school curriculum—to be worked in between band practice and social dance, time permitting.

Primarily, the textbook should be a factual survey of the subject matter in its entirety and should provide a perspective. Serving this function, the textbook gives the teacher time to arouse the student's interest, to direct his attention to deeper analysis, to guide him in the method and materials appropriate to the analysis, and to introduce the generalizations, details, and understandings that make the analysis meaningful. Thus, the roles of the history teacher and the history textbook are clearly distinct—that of the text is basic but subordinate in the total instructional process.

In high school teaching, the history instructor must see to it that the necessary overview is provided. It is unrealistic to assume that the student's pre-high school instruction in American history will serve as an adequate foundation from which the teacher may spring blithely into advanced considerations—a course of action much more agreeable to the teacher as a history major, but most often entirely inappropriate to the circumstances.

Nor does the proposed interpretations approach, with its library and classroom investigation of a number of the most carefully selected topics representing the major phases of American history, constitute, of itself, a coverage of American history. The need for a narrative thread remains. The nature of the interpretations approach, with its emphasis upon specified reading selections and investigation of primary source materials, suggests that almost any text that provides a reliable survey of American history should be adequate. In establishing the factual foundation, of course, some are more reliable than others.

With multiple copies of dependable general texts on reserve in the library, the need of each student for a standard textbook is greatly reduced, though not eliminated. What is effectively disposed of by the interpretations approach is the need for a uniform text for all students. This affords a student the opportunity to provide himself with whatever text or texts are best suited to him. The teacher should provide a list of inexpensive, dependable texts and should describe the function that the text is to serve, so that the student is disposed to judge the merits of each of the possibilities available. The text should provide a factual account, without necessarily becoming encyclopedic in detail. For an interpretations approach to selected topics, the text should be organized on a chronological, rather than on a topical, basis. The Barnes and Noble College Outline Series *American History at a Glance,* or narrative accounts such as Allan Nevins and Henry S. Commager's *Pocket History of the United States* (Washington Square), William Miller's *History of the United States* (Dell), and similar works are admirably suited to providing the needed idea of sequence and perspective.

Because of widespread misconception of the function of the textbook, it has been impressed to serve needs far beyond the reach of its capacity to satisfy, with the result that it has received much criticism for nonperformance. A textbook is not American history, nor is it a course in American history.

Yet, when the role of the textbook is properly understood, there is mounting suspicion, among teachers and publishers alike, that that institution has outgrown its own usefulness (few American history textbooks issued or revised since 1950 number fewer than 750 large pages), and that its successor is becoming more and more firmly established.

The collection of paperbacks by high school libraries and by individual students numbers several overwhelming advantages; among them are economy, variety, and scholarship. If the student is going to read 750 pages (and if the school is going to provide him with 750 pages of reading), the material might just as well be inexpensive, interesting, and worth reading.

Reluctance on the part of high school departments to embrace the paperback completely stems from many sources, few of which are defensible: from "textbook teachers" who "have always done it this way," preferring covering textbooks to preparing reading lists or familiarizing themselves with new materials; from departmental economic commitments to make use of what they have and what they have ordered for the following year (*ad infinitum*); from the unreasoning lurking misapprehension that the school must provide general-issue texts or it has no truly public system of education. It will take time to bring a change long overdue, and in the meantime the standard textbook, the high school student, and American history will stand abused.

STUDENT-OWNED MATERIALS

The ideal learning situation, from the point of view of both teacher and student, is that in which every student has his own copy of whatever is being studied. In the proposed course or any course that makes use of a great variety of different sources, this is not possible. However, required readings should be readily available and accessible to the students. This is a matter of immediate concern to the high school teacher, since, at that level particularly, the student is easily discouraged by what quickly becomes an exasperating quest for a book, and he is very likely never to renew the first effort. The degree of availability of source material to the student conditions the success of the interpretations approach. That approach depends upon the library collection to guarantee a uniform opportunity of study to all students, many of whom, however, soon discover the advantages of having a personal copy of at least the basic titles. Student purchases should be encouraged, since this relieves pressure on both the time-pressed student and the library's limited capacity to meet his demands. The student's private investment and personal acquisition serve to sharpen his interest in the purchase, and he is at once aware of the other privileges of private ownership: the freedom of underscoring, of marking up, and of making marginal notations as he likes.

Emphatically, student purchase of books, especially paperbacks, is not unrealistic nonsense. School bookstores, stocked with realistic and readable history, are becoming more and more common. Many teachers are maintaining classroom collections of secondhand paperbacks. Increasingly, the student is coming to provide his own books as they become more readily available to him. This is a very healthy state of affairs which allows the teacher to be more constructive and to investigate the avalanche of less expensive resources, evaluating their usefulness in terms of students and course, and bringing them to the attention of the class.

The final phase of investigation in the proposed course focuses upon that outside reading that places each unit problem within the setting of its time, or suggests corollaries or contradictions that may either clarify or further obscure its resolution. The instructor may attempt to provide these readings at least in part, through the circulating library, if the library happens to represent a better collection than most do. The enterprising teacher may seize the opportunity provided by final phase considerations to wean the students away from the school library and introduce them to the personal library notion. It may well be their last opportunity. History teachers must tap the power of generating interest that lies in the paperback bookstore. The high school student's awakened interest in bookstore browsing, in selecting and reading the books that are within his means, is the surest indication of his having been successfully introduced to history on a lifetime basis.

The lists of paperbacks found in Appendix B includes only those works directly related to the problem advanced in each unit of this particular course proposal. It cannot include all of the titles of interest and, as the selection of unit problems varies with the individual teacher, so too will the selection of readings. Though many other works important to the illumination of many problems do not appear in paperbound editions at present, in deference to the limited means of the average high school student, only those that do are listed here. It should be noted that schools frequently maintain their own bookstore and stock the less expensive volumes, while the library concentrates upon those works available only in hard cover—a sound procedure that the history teacher might find instructive.

Four: Classroom Procedures in the Interpretations Approach

Even amid plentiful resources, many attempts to initiate problems courses in social studies at the high school level have proved unworkable, foundered, and collapsed. In any problems approach, the student must have (1) a clear understanding of what the problem is; (2) an explicit understanding of how it is to be resolved; and, deriving from these two, (3) confidence in himself and in his teacher. The idea of the problems approach, as in any other approach, is not to bewilder, but to enlighten; not to confuse and scatter, but to draw together and clarify. These are the requisites of success; the key is structure. Sound problems organization requires first, careful structuring of the problem itself, and second, careful mobilization of the resources involved in approaching it.

STRUCTURE

The process of posing the problem, at the high school level, must take into account the student's lack of a frame of reference. For all intents and purposes the junior high school course has not provided him with a foundation in the subject matter of American history upon which the high school teacher can build with confidence. Moreover, he has had little or no experience in analyzing reading selections for their key points, and much less experience in analyzing historical interpretations for their central arguments. He has neither a framework of information nor any idea of how to develop or organize one.

For this reason it is not enough to provide each student in the class with an assignment sheet upon which have been typed the words, "Was the American Revolution a struggle against tyranny or an unfortunate accident?" Such a question may afford him an idea of the general concern of the problem, but does not define it. The same assignment given to a graduate history major might summon to his mind at once a framework of reference—bibliography and preliminary analyses. Such is not the case with eleventh or twelfth graders.

For them, the central question must be broken down into its component parts, and the relationship of each part must be defined and explained. Thus, sub-questions to the major questions should be provided as an outline of the two conflicting positions:

I. *Was the American Revolution a struggle against tyranny or an unfortunate accident?*

A. Was the British economic policy a just one?

B. Were the political principles of Britain and of her colonies irreconcilably different?

C. Was the American Revolution primarily an internal struggle for social supremacy?

Very much in order is the lecture that explains the problem in terms of its historic and historiographic setting, that points out the varying implications of tyranny—economic, political and social—and defines "unfortunate accident." The structuring of the problem continues:

A. Was the British economic policy a just one?

1. Did the British mercantile system operate to mutual advantage?
2. Did Parliament levy unjust taxes?

and further:

1. Did the British mercantile system operate to mutual advantage?
a. in trade regulation?
b. in industry regulation?

Carried to this length, the structuring of the problem is complete. The student's lack of background has been anticipated and provided for; his doubts as to what he is to do have been resolved. He has an idea of both the problem's expanse and some of its facets; he understands it in terms of its major concern, its integral component parts, and their relation to one another. The problem is clear. He is confident and ready to move to detailed evidence for its solution.

The process of structuring is completed by relating the specific readings, chapter and verse, to those precise problems to which each has application. This requires a familiarity with sources and a willingness to work. It is at this point, if not earlier, that the teacher often decides in unfortunate indolence that the development of "independent study" is more important.

In the interpretations approach presented here, excerpts from reading selections have been inserted among the major questions and sub-questions to further define and illustrate the conflicting viewpoints. These should suggest to the student an angle of attack, though most often teacher assistance in an analysis is necessary. At first, training in the development of research techniques should not include any problem in locating the sources. They should be identified for him and be made readily available to his immediate use. At the beginning, especially, the greater detail of citation (page references) of that treatment relating to a specific part of the problem is very desirable. It is recommended that such source references be listed on the mimeographed assignment sheet next to the appropriate topic. The high school student will have enough to do in concentrating upon what is said, without the additional burden of learning where to find it. The point is history, not mystery.

A competent historic and historiographic overview of each topic is recommended to provide a common basis of beginning. Further, a list of related readings, on a unit-by-unit basis, is appropriate; readings organized on a detailed problem-by-problem basis are of greater value than a general and miscellaneous list. Such organization requires teacher familiarity with the resources available in the school library as well as at nearby bookstores that stock paperbacks.

As suggested in another part of this study, there is no need for launching the entire program. Doing one unit well requires considerable expenditure of time and energy.

THE FUNCTION OF THE TEACHER

In a chapter devoted to "Former Students," Irwin Edman, late Professor of Philosophy in Columbia College, appraised the relationship of the classroom teacher to the process of learning:

> It is not what the teacher but what the world teaches them that will in the long run count, and what they can learn from the latter comes from habits fixed soon after birth and temperaments fixed long before it. There are just a few things a teacher can do, and that only for the sensitive and spirited. He can initiate enthusiasms, clear paths, and inculcate discipline. He can communicate a passion and a method, no more. His most serious triumph as a teacher is the paradoxical one of having his students, while he is teaching them and perhaps afterwards, forget him in the absorption of the tradition or the inquiry of which he is the transient voice. Lucky for him if later his students feel his voice was just. As in the playing of music, it is the music, not the musician, that is ultimate. And in the art of teaching, it is what is taught that counts, not the teacher. It is a great tribute to an artist to say that he plays Beethoven or Bach, and puts nothing between them and his audience.

But in so doing he becomes one with both the composer and the listener. In the listener's memory he anonymously shares the composer's immortality. The teacher, too, is best remembered who is thus forgotten. He lives in what has happened to the minds of his students, and in what they remember of these things infinitely greater than themselves or than himself.[1]

Though in classroom practice the teacher's communication of method and of passion are not disjointed operations, for purposes of convenience they will be treated here as separate considerations.

The teacher's effort to communicate the method of history is discernible in three parts corresponding to the three distinct phases of the interpretations approach.

INTRODUCTORY PHASE

In Phase I, in which the problem is presented and analyzed, the first function of the teacher is one of introduction. The teacher must provide the students with the historical background, which should suggest the historical significance of the question itself, arousing greater interest than it would if the event in question were some isolated phenomenon. The teacher also introduces a panoramic view of the older and newer interpretations of the particular question. The most suitable form of presentation of the problem and its historical setting and interpretations seems to be the lecture, which is used to greatest advantage in situations where the class has little or no information and needs sweeping coverage in ordered form. In presenting this introductory material, the teacher should make use of reading assignments of a general nature, texts for factual survey and overviews of interpretations.

In introductory units of the interpretations approach, the teacher must be careful to focus the students' attention upon two conflicting opinions, generalizing all that have been introduced, and reducing them to two positions. The teacher need not be reminded of the dangers of over-simplification—an occupational hazard—but it is essential to build the self-assurance that comes with clarity, leaving the complexities to reveal themselves as the analysis progresses. While the psychological interpretation of the impact of propaganda as a cause of the American Revolution has a distinct niche among the historical viewpoints, it can be incorporated into the "unfortunate accident" argument without conjuring the spectre of Procrustes. The instance of multiple causality of the Civil War reduces logically to two: avoidable or irrepressible conflict. The relating of each separate interpretation to one or the other camp increases the students' understanding of all positions. With some

[1] Irwin Edman, *Philosopher's Holiday* (New York: Viking, 1938), p. 123.

experience, students should be able to provide their own groupings, which may at times conflict, offering ideal possibilities for the final phase-concluding discussions.

Having reduced all interpretations to two, the next step in the introductory phase is to pinpoint the key arguments upon which each of the conflicting interpretations rests. The teacher should direct a classroom analysis and enumeration of those specific arguments that support each case and that will be the subject of the succeeding library investigation.

The idea of dividing the class into two or more groups, each to investigate different aspects of the problem, suggests itself at once; however, though individual successes may suggest the contrary, the general practice is fraught with risk. High school students have repeatedly demonstrated that one thing of less interest to them than the teacher's opinion is that of their classmates. The oral reports of even the brightest students grow wearisome. Each student should be held responsible for the entire coverage of the introductory considerations, for in the concluding class presentations it is important that every student be evaluating the same arguments. This suggests mimeographed handouts which structure the problem in sub-questions. Accompanying the problem outlines should be the reading lists, naming and directing the students' use to specific sources. The teacher may elect to restrict the use of primary sources until the secondary opinions have been digested, with a view toward demonstrating the respective value of each.

LIBRARY INVESTIGATION PHASE

The library investigation phase imposes two obligations upon the teacher. First, he must guide the students to the proper resources of the library, coordinating his efforts, whenever possible, with those of the librarian. Order is the key to successful use of the library. It has been greatly advanced by providing each student with a clear statement of the problem and a list of the specific sources wherein he may expect to find answers. Having the class assemble in the library rather than in the classroom first saves precious time, limits confusion, and eliminates the atmosphere of informality which develops in moving large numbers of students from one place to another. Each student should have a designated place and be in that place when the bell rings. If the library situation is such that it is possible to have those works to be used at once on a table, rather than on the shelf, library output is further increased—especially if they need not be replaced at the end of the period. The minimal in-school reading time is a weakness of the interpretations approach and conservation of it is imperative. Saving eight minutes of time that is often needlessly wasted in the use of the library represents a saving of a full period each week.

In addition to reading, students will be taking notes and synthesizing information. The teacher must make himself available on an individual basis, to direct students in the investigation process. He may find it necessary to call a class meeting for progress reports when a difficulty arises which appears to be common. Such might have great value, not only in providing relief in a period of four weeks of library research, but also in providing necessary encouragement and confidence.

The teacher's personal overseeing and direction on an individual basis in reading copy, making needed corrections and suggestions, viewing outlines, screening relevant and irrelevant materials, is of inestimable value, and one which growing school systems ordinarily have been unable to provide.

CONCLUDING PHASE

In the final phase, the teacher's major functions are to evaluate student achievement, to draw conclusions on each major question, and to propose new lines of approach and new materials which suggest the uninterrupted nature of history.

The teacher appoints students to submit final reports to the class that state their conclusions. He appoints and directs the preparation of critiques of the major papers, readily noting the rise of controversial or confusing issues during the topic's investigation that suggests the depth and complexity of the problem, or leads to a clearer understanding of it as a basis for concluding assignments. The teacher schedules the reports, determines the mode of presentation, leads in evaluating organization and presentation, and guides class questioning to the crucial issues.

The judgment of the teacher may be required. He must be prepared to evaluate the evidence presented, praise what is good, condemn what is wrong, make further contributions to what has been established, and suggest new ideas and materials. The teacher may make use of the final considerations for providing transitional materials linking the completed unit with the next. An analysis of the Declaration of Independence for its statement of causes of the American Revolution is easily converted to an analysis of the same document for its statement of freedom, which, in the arrangement presented in this proposal, serves as a basis for the next unit—"The Constitution: Rejection or Reaffirmation of the Declaration of Independence?"

In communicating this method of history to the student, the teacher must command his confidence, must simplify at the beginning and complicate at the end, while avoiding both oversimplification and student frustration.

COURSE ASSIGNMENTS

While it is important for the history teacher to bear in mind that history is not only read but is also written, and that the assignments must therefore attend to the development of both skills, the interpretations approach stresses the need for extraordinary reading. Though heavy in its demands, however, the nature of the approach does offer compensating features. When these are taken into account and when lesser sacrifices can be made in other areas, the requirements upon student time and energy of the proposed course are seen to be well within the bounds of reason.

At the outset, an important psychological advantage obtains in eliminating the coverage of a textbook as a course objective. The function of texts is shifted from that of bible to that of reference work. It should be used only as needed—a much more enjoyable situation than one of responsibility for total content. The reading that is done in its place is varied and personally useful, not to say exciting and entertaining. Much of the student's enjoyment of his assignments, of course, depends upon his teacher. Few teachers, however inspirational, can make a textbook "go."

Another advantageous feature which accrues because of the nature of the approach, is the de-emphasis of the need for recall. Rather, the objective of the interpretations approach focuses upon the development of understandings.

Aside from its additional implications for abandoning the textbook, the reduced emphasis upon recall suggests the diminished use or elimination of conventional examinations, attended by cramming activities which have little lasting value. The time and energy expended by students in preparation for exams can be put to much more valuable use. They represent, ordinarily, a tremendous number of clock hours.

Finally, de-emphasizing the need for recall should indicate the advantage of sacrificing the nightly "busy work" assignments that are not uncommon. To all intents and purposes, student effort in looking up and writing out answers to questions at the end of chapters yields little of either recall or understanding of history. Completion of such homework is not even a guarantee that the student has read the material. This points up the value of this type of assignment for developing the skill of skim-reading which most often, unfortunately, is not the desired intent. If the assignment is to have value, the student must know its purpose. Assignments for which the purpose is not clear or for which, as often happens, there is no purpose, are better eliminated.

In most instances of homework overload, the problem is to be found not in total weight of work assigned but in uneven distribution of that weight in terms of time. The interpretations approach requires continuous preparation and does not lend itself to being put off until the last minute. In so doing, it offers a possibility of distribution of effort which will lighten the load, though the total weight may be greater. The amount of work done in the eleventh hour by a high school student would be negligible when spread out over the course of a week.

Finally it must be remembered that much of the required work of the proposed interpretations approach is to be done during scheduled class time, and with direct teacher supervision.

The assignments related to the problem-introduction phase are of both mandatory and optional character. All students are responsible for an understanding of the historic setting of the problem and a familiarity with the basic interpretations related to it. Since they are responsible for understanding a topic rather than for the content of a specified number of pages, the weight of the assignment varies. Some may consult six sources or authorities on the subject of the Alien and Sedition Acts; some may see only one account. The basic reading which serves to provide the overview of interpretations must be studied carefully. The readings prescribed in connection with the proposed units number less than twenty-five pages—three or four pages each night in addition to reviewing lectures notes. Two basic reading selections average twenty-five pages. They demonstrate the two conflicting viewpoints, which are to be analyzed for their major arguments (with teacher supervision). The entire reading requirement for this introduction phase, where it appears in bulk, and for which there is no written work required, numbers about ten pages per school night. Reading lists together with optional assignments to be presented in the third phase are appropriately distributed during the first week of consideration of each topic. Individual or committee reports on selected topics related to the problem or reviews of major books and articles, of which there may be only a single copy, suggest themselves as valuable optional assignments. Command of the basic information and understandings is the responsibility of all.

The second phase of the assignment requires a moving out into varied readings, primary and secondary sources, and the preparation of a written statement of conclusions drawn from the evidence examined by each student. Each should prepare his report with the probability of his being called upon to present his views in the final phase. The student or students who are to give their reports orally may not be designated until the last minute. It is further suggested that the required length of the report be determined by its adequacy as defined by the class. Assigning a specific number of pages defeats the purpose, and suggests the subordination of its true purpose to interests of "busy work." Mimeographed instructions which define the adequacy and other requirements of the paper should be distributed and posted in the library and the classroom.

The concluding phase need not carry any formal assignment of its own, although the teacher may determine that some additional reading is necessary to the maturation of considerations. It is recommended that students be left free to present opinions formally or informally, and to advance their personal interests.

It is suggested that the reports presented deal with the specific sub-questions, thereby affording the student further opportunity to realize the significance of each piece of evidence. Moreover, this method impresses the understanding of each detail, develops the idea of complexity, and gives rise to controversy. Also, from a practical standpoint, more students participate.

COURSE TESTING AND EVALUATION

Some theorists who are less familiar with the high school classroom, particularly those devoted to theorizing on the instruction of honor students, have expressed a concern that high school students dislike or even fear testing, and that the performance of honor students in particular is even cramped by it. Any form of evaluation is a time-consuming process, but evaluation serves very important functions which are sometimes mistakenly dispensed with at the honor level with damaging effect.

Continuous evaluation provides constant diagnoses of teacher and student progress; it forces production, which makes it indispensable to teaching honors or any other classes; and, contrary to the trauma-producing properties with which it is often credited, it serves the students with constant and up-to-date information on their standing. This is important to all, though particularly so to honor students. The results weigh the disadvantages, and it is necessary to the efficacy of any high of regular evaluation are not only desirable, but its advantages far out-school offering.

As suggested above, the inadequacies of the major examination as the suitable method of evaluating accomplishment in the interpretations course are apparent. Whatever device is employed, it must reflect the objectives of the course, which in the present case stress the development of skills and understandings. Accordingly, while periodic quizzing is necessary to one phase of the interpretations approach, the weight of evaluation rests upon the preparation and presentation of formal papers setting forth an account of the method used and the results obtained.

Since the specific objectives of the first phase include the promotion of student familiarity with history subject matter and a number of interpretations, frequent use of the spot quiz is recommended. It is essential that the student's level of understanding of the problem's background be clearly diagnosed before moving into the library-investigation phase for its solution. Daily quizzing during the first phase also encourages students to apply themselves constantly to the study needed to gain the necessary command. Quizzes given during the first few days should aim at checking on comprehension of the conflicting interpretations presented in lectures. Such quizzes might require students to identify the authors of selected excerpts, or to identify which of the conflicting viewpoints each of a series of statements supports. The last day of the first phase may then be set aside for a quiz testing the command of factual information on the topic. Students might be held responsible for summarizing a different source's account each day.

The work being done in the library during the second phase does provide the teacher with the opportunity for continued evaluation of the individual, checking his reading ability, his use of the library, his familiarity with different sources, his method of taking notes, and his powers of analysis and synthesis.

It might be suggested that the teacher make no formal evaluation in the course of the second phase. The teacher is in constant touch with each student so that the need for diagnosis is satisfied; moreover, the atmosphere of freedom and independent study is as important to the student's development as teacher supervision, which seems to accomplish much more when framed in an advisory capacity.

The third phase offers opportunity for the most valid and constructive evaluation, the presentation of the finished product in which the student demonstrates his familiarity with the topic, with its interpretations, and with the sources. He shows his willingness to work, his diligence in marshaling evidence, his care in evaluating it, and his ability to draw the reasonable conclusions, to synthesize, to present, and to defend it.

The class's evaluation of the work of its individual members serves a useful purpose in setting the standards of expectation and quality, standards which, most infrequently, the teacher is compelled to alter in favor of mercy.

Some important aspects of evaluation relate to intangibles, not revealed by paper-and-pencil tests. Voluntary reading, exploration of by-paths, questions that reflect thought, doubts, challenges, or aroused curiosity—all characteristics of movement toward independent study— offer better evidence of the success of the interpretations approach than examinations ordinarily provide. Such qualitative responses depend largely on the motivation that characterizes good teaching.

MOTIVATION

As the teacher introduces the student to the study of history and initiates him in the use of its method and tools, he cannot help but impart his own interest and enthusiasm for his field. In conjunction with communication of the method goes communication of the passion, appearing the more important of the two. The man with the passion for history though untutored in its method is of far more use to himself than he who, versed in method, is wanting in passion. The enthusiastic teacher is an inspiration to his students, and the power to introduce the student to the study of history on a lasting basis resides in the communication, not of the method, but of the passion, of the power to inspire.

The proposed interpretations approach possesses four major intrinsic features which contribute to the inspiration of the student. First, the course revolves around conflicting opinion which in itself is a source of interest. Teachers from the beginning have made use of controversy to prod flagging interest, taking care that the energy produced by conflict generates more light than heat. The conflict approach must be attended by the development of skills in critical thinking, or it is used to no purpose.

Second, through its solution-seeking nature, any problems course, including this, provides a purpose for study. The high school student not only understands his work and its value, but appreciates the more mature, sophisticated approach.

Third, the interpretations approach and other problems approaches which demand greater latitude and depth in reading afford the student the opportunity to discover and explore areas of personal interest of which he might have remained unaware.

Finally, the interpretations approach or any carefully structured problems approach develops and maintains the student's confidence, suggests the pleasures rather than the drudgery of reading, analysis, and investigations, and moves him toward independent study.

Five: Implications of the Interpretations Approach to American History in High School

The implications of the proposed interpretations approach are various and far-reaching, taking in considerations of school administrators, boards of education, curriculum directors, guidance personnel, and those charged with programmng students, librarians, many teachers, most students, and parents. They involve budgets, public-relations policies, state and national testing procedures, the merits of "tracking" or grouping students, and a host of other considerations, all of which may be important at one time or another but which serve to distract attention from the central idea. The present discussion of the implications of the interpretations approach is confined, therefore, to its most basic usefulness: that relating to the teacher and to the student of American history in the high school.

FOR TEACHERS

This study's attempt to explore the possibilities of teaching American history at the high school level through the writings of its interpreters grew out of a high school teacher's increasing concern, as he moved deeper and deeper into his subject area through continued study and teaching, at finding himself more and more unresolved as to what exactly should be presented in the classroom. Many teachers, impervious to the existence of sharply conflicting viewpoints involving subject matter, simply lead the students through the text and let them sleep undisturbed. Others, mildly suspicious of the depth and complexity of history, gingerly pick their way down a "middle road" and entertain themselves with illusions of objectivity. Yet, the obligation of intellectual honesty that binds both researchers and teachers requires of them continuing investigation and a truly objective presentation. The teacher has the added responsibility of demonstrating the value of the fruits of research and of encouraging continued interest in knowledge.

In the process of guiding his students in the steps of historical research, the teacher is communicating to them, at the same time, his own personal appreciation of and enthusiasm for history and the historical method. The enthusiastic teacher is an inspiration to his students, generating and developing in them an interest in the subject matter that may some day surpass his own. In the final analysis, it is the arousing of the student's interest in history that is the teacher's most fundamental and most important task.

There is no justification for the teacher to assume that he has never satisfied his personal or teaching needs when he has mastered the essentials, nor is there any excuse for his failure to present contradictory evidence and controversy in order to preserve his own intellectual comfort or that of his students. Where such comfort exists there is neither teaching nor learning.

> A parent gives life, but as parent, gives no more. A murderer takes life but his deed stops there. A teacher affects eternity; he can never tell where his influence stops. A teacher is expected to teach truth, and may perhaps flatter himself that he does so, if he stops with the alphabet or the multiplication table, as a mother teaches truth by making her child eat with a spoon; but morals are quite another truth and philosophy is more complex still. A teacher must either treat history as a catalogue, a record, a romance, or as an evolution; and whether he affirms or denies evolution, he falls into all the burning faggots of the pit. He makes of his scholars either priests or atheists, plutocrats or socialists, judges or anarchists, almost in spite of himself. In essence incoherent and immoral, history had either to be taught as such—or falsified.[1]

When history is presented in its incoherence, complexity, and conflict, as in the proposed interpretations approach, the teacher must make certain that the student is prepared to deal with it as such. When the nature of history is introduced, the use of the historical method must be introduced along with it, and the inseparability of the two must be clearly demonstrated. The teacher who undertakes to present the interpretations approach must have, in addition to good control of subject matter—the historical information, its sources, and its major interpretations—a working command of historical method. He must be prepared to demonstrate its use, its application, and its form. He must be able to evaluate the methods of research and criticism employed by the students whom he has taught and to encourage what is sound and destroy what is slovenly in their techniques. Presentation of the interpretations approach requires development, and in some cases resurrection, of a third dimension in high school teachers as well as in high school stu-

---

[1] Henry Adams, *The Education of Henry Adams* (Boston: Houghton Mifflin, 1918), pp. 300–301.

dents. Teachers are provided with an opportunity to continue growing indefinitely and to make use of their own studies in the classroom.

Additionally, two very practical implications for the classroom teacher must be considered in viewing the potential of the interpretations approach. The teacher is unfortunately subject to outside pressures that may determine what he presents and how he presents it. There is plentiful evidence that problems arise when controversial issues are broached in social studies classes. The teacher will do well to anticipate protests to any suggestion that the American Revolution was fought for any reason other than as a struggle against tyranny, that the Civil War was a needless conflict produced by a "blundering generation," or that Franklin Roosevelt sold out to the Soviets at the Yalta Conference. Such protests are an index to the general need for training in the historical method. In satisfying this need, the teacher renders an important service to the community. Use of the sources of history, together with analysis both of differing interpretations and of the bases of the differences, protects the teacher against misunderstanding of his motives and involves students in education rather than in possible indoctrination.

The classroom teacher must be freed from the various official and unofficial entanglements that presently restrain him from getting the preparation he needs and the opportunity he wants to teach history. It is not the intention of this discussion to suggest that every teacher is a chained Prometheus awaiting release to embark upon heroic adventures, but to point up restrictions which are unnecessarily discouraging many fine students who might have chosen teaching and many fine teachers who could be more effective. The proposed approach, properly put into effect and maintained in action, is guaranteed to keep the teacher alive and stimulated.

FOR STUDENTS

Few teachers of history have selected this particular field because they sought to change their lives or illuminate their futures. Few have followed Clio with a view to enlarging their capacity for citizenship or perfecting its fulfillment. Few are converted to its study by a sudden soul-searching revelation of prejudice, intolerance, or even myopia within themselves. Yet these are the major reasons, according to the lists of "objectives" produced by professional aim formulators, why high school students must undertake a study of history. Proceeding with a study of history on the basis of such values is the most monstrous thing yet perpetrated against either children or history. It becomes clear why many students remain unenthusiastic and even hostile to the study of history. Most history teachers have chosen the field because they are interested in history and because they like it. Like poetry, history, if it is to be brought successfully to the attention of others, must be introduced to them on the basis of its own intrinsic merit. One thing the least advanced thirteen-year-old mind can do quickly is to see through the carefully contrived correlation of citizenship and history as a demonstration of the latter's importance. The seventeen-year-old is even more sophisticated. Since the intrinsic and undefinable appeal of history is what has attracted students, teachers, and citizens down through the centuries, it seems reasonable that this appeal might be the more appropriate and the more successful approach in introducing the student to Clio. Indeed it seems the only one.

History, left to itself, will not attract the interest of all students. This is a perfectly natural phenomenon. The devotees of history, like those devoted to Beethoven or Degas, are ardent, but comparatively few in number. Democratic education does require that the opportunity to appreciate history, music, art, and literature be provided to all. No system of education can reasonably expect that the students' response to this opportunity will be equal. The subject matter cannot be so diluted as to appeal successfully to society's lowest common denominator. Even though the idea is advanced with the finest intentions of humane egalitarians, it works an injustice to the integrity of the subject matter (which is not preserved by insistence upon "total coverage"), strips it of the muscle that might appeal to the more capable student, and even manages to offend those among the benighted who have insight enough to realize that they are being insulted. The opportunity to appreciate history must be presented without corruption of the subject. How valuable is an acquaintance or interest that has been cultivated under false pretenses? The history teacher, examining his own introduction to history, and his growing appreciation of it, must be willing to rely upon that same power of attraction inherent in the study of history to win more friends among his students. What he must do is guarantee that they are introduced in such a way they clearly understand one another. Students must be given an opportunity to *study* history rather than to skim its surface.

High school is for some students preparation for college; for others it is terminal. In either case the opportunity for introducing the student to the study of history should not be missed. The high school course may serve as the basis of advanced course work or of a well-grounded, pleasurable personal interest. Regardless of the nature of the follow-up, the formal introduction to the study of history must be a proper one.

Clearly understood, the favorite dispute as to whether the controlling aim of teaching history at the high school level should be one of providing breadth or depth, coverage or understanding, practically resolves itself. The difference between "coverage" and depth approaches is seen to be one of degree, not of kind. The historical evolutionists believe that the importance of coverage is defined in terms of piecing together all of the fragments of man's past which will yield an understanding of ourselves. This is a remarkably vain approach to history. Notwithstanding this, a value of coverage does in fact exist in providing the student with the widest possible field in which to locate an interest. A student who is bored by the ancient Greeks may be fascinated by modern revolutions. One recent student in an American history course who was not able to muster enough enthusiasm to maintain a passing grade through the first semester suddenly astonished the teacher with his literacy in an effort reading "problem" and continued to go to the reading clinic faithfully to feed a fierce interest in the American Civil War. The student had a reading "problem" and continued to go to the reading clinic faithfully, though in a few weeks he had exhausted the works of Bruce Catton, which he bought, and a fairly sizeable collection on the Civil War in the high school library. The importance of coverage receives undue emphasis in situations where it is conceived as a value in itself; coverage for the sake of coverage looms particularly large in New York State, where the one-year courses in world history and American history are followed by State Regents examinations. Such examinations are useful in assuring the latitude to students, but not infrequently the teacher must sacrifice the depth necessary for proper introduction to chronological breadth. At this point, as classroom teachers realize, the treatment becomes so superficial that coverage itself does not in fact exist.

The interpretations approach incorporates the one value of coverage with the depth necessary not only to make the particular area meaningful but also to provide the student with a view of the complex nature of all history. Thus, a combination of coverage and depth is effected on the basis of selection—which, it should be remembered, also serves as the basis of compiling the most comprehensive "coverage" offered by any course or textbook.

As a final consideration of the implications of the proposed approach for the student it should be noted that this approach provides him with a real opportunity to become interested in, and to pursue, a study of history. It gives him the topics of inquiry selected on the basis of significance and interest. It supplies him with a carefully structured plan of approach that should maintain his confidence, a familiarity with the methods and tools of the study of history and personal direction in their use, and a program of evaluation in which his success or failure

75

is at once evident. It furnishes the student with an opportunity for pursuit of interest or curiosity which, like history itself, has no limits. Students generally considered to be of "average" or "below average" ability are going through high school without ever being made aware that they might enjoy history, because they are grouped into low-performance castes where nothing is going on and where nothing is expected of them. Guidance personnel define their capacity and interest to the fourth decimal place and set corresponding standards of expectation at low levels. The teachers concur in the conspiracy as does the obliging average student who conforms by endeavoring to be average and the below average student by being below average.

Since its concepts should be—and can be—applied at all levels in the high school study of history, the interpretations approach to history seems to offer a possibility of revolutionizing the teaching of history throughout the high school. More important, since it concentrates upon providing the student with a distinct frame of reference through presenting major conflicting interpretations, and with the historical method proper to the study of history, it is hoped that the interpretations approach in the high school will rejuvenate in future generations a genuine interest in American history.

Appendix A: Sources of American History in Paperback

The list in this appendix and in Appendix B following should provide the classroom teacher with an idea of the materials available at comparatively low cost for building a collection in American history consisting of documents, readings, and interpretations, and ranging from general history to special areas. This collection is capable of sustaining the proposed approach in its entirety or in part. Any titles referred to specifically in the text are marked with an asterisk (*) and those of special interest with a dagger (†).

Each title is listed in its most recently available edition. A few of the entries, marked with a double dagger (‡), were out of print at the time this manuscript went to press, but may still be available in bookstores or may soon be in print again.

DOCUMENTS AND READINGS IN GENERAL AMERICAN HISTORY

Billington, Ray A., B. J. Loewenberg, S. H. Brockunier, and D. S. Sparks (eds.), *The Making of American Democracy: Readings and Documents* (rev. ed), 2 vols. New York: Holt, Rinehart & Winston, Inc.

Bryce, James, *Reflections on American Institutions.* New York: Fawcett World Library (Premier Books).

Commager, Henry S. (ed.), *Documents of American History,* 2 vols. New York: Appleton-Century-Crofts.

Cotner, Robert C., G. C. Fite, and J. S. Ezell (eds.), *Readings in American History* (3rd ed.), Vol. II. Boston: Houghton Mifflin Co.

Current, Richard N. and J. A. Garraty (eds.), *Words That Made American History,* 2 vols. Boston: Little, Brown & Co.

Ezell, J. S., *et al.* (ed.), *Readings in American History* (3rd ed.), Vol. I. Boston: Houghton Mifflin Co.

Freidel, Frank and Norman Pollack (eds.), *Builders of American Institutions.* Chicago: Rand McNally & Co.

Heffner, Richard D. (ed.), *A Documentary History of the United States.* New York: New American Library (Mentor Books).

Hofstadter, Richard (ed.), *Great Issues in American History,* 2 vols. New York: Random House, Inc. (Vintage Books).

Hollingsworth, J. Rogers and B. Wiley (eds.), *American Democracy: A Documentary Record,* 2 vols. New York: Thomas Y. Crowell.

Huszar, George B. and H. W. Littlefield, *Basic American Documents.* Totowa, N. J.: Littlefield, Adams & Co.

Levy, L. and Merrill Peterson, *Major Crises in American History: Documentary Problems,* 2 vols. New York: Harcourt, Brace & World.

Meyers, Marvin, A. Kern, and J. G. Cawelti (eds.), *Sources of the American Republic,* 2 vols. Glenview, Ill.: Scott, Foresman & Co.

Morris, Richard B. (ed.), *Basic Documents in American History.* Princeton, N. J.: D. Van Nostrand Co., Inc.

Readings in American History, 15 vols. Chicago: Rand McNally & Co.

The Creation of Society in the New World, S. Diamond

Rebel Versus Tory: The Crises of the Revolution, 1773–1776, J. T. Main

The Puritan in the Enlightenment: Franklin and Edwards, D. Levin

Adams and Jefferson: "Posterity Must Judge," A. Koch

Andrew Jackson, Nullification and the States-Rights Tradition, C. G. Sellers

Abolitionism: Disrupter of the Democratic System or Agent of Progress?, B. A. Weisberger

The Secession Crisis, 1860–1861, P. J. Staudenraus

Reconstruction and the Freedmen, G. McWhiney

Science and the Emergence of Modern America: 1865–1916, A. H. Dupree

The Issue of Federal Regulation in the Progressive Era, R. M. Abrams

The Coming of War, 1917, E. R. May

The Discontent of the Intellectuals: A Problem of the Twenties, H. May

Labor and the New Deal, E. D. Cronon

Conscience, Science and Security: The Case of Dr. J. Robert Oppenheimer, C. Strout

The Cold War: Containment and Its Critics, H. Ross

Stourzh, Gerald and R. Lerner (eds.), *Readings in American Democracy* (rev. ed). New York: Oxford University Press.

Syrett, Harold C. (ed.), *American Historical Documents.* New York: Barnes & Noble, Inc.

Tryon, Warren S. (ed.) *My Native Land: Life in America, 1790–1870.* Chicago: University of Chicago Press (Phoenix Books).

DOCUMENTS AND READINGS IN SPECIAL AREAS OF AMERICAN HISTORY

‡Aptheker, Herbert (ed.), *Documentary History of the Negro People in the United States* (rev. ed). New York: International Publishers.

Billington, Ray A. (ed.), *Frontier and Section: Selected Essays of Frederick Jackson Turner.* Englewood Cliffs, N. J.: Prentice-Hall, Inc. (Spectrum Books).

Billington, Ray A., *Westward Movement in the United States.* Princeton, N. J.: D. Van Nostrand Co., Inc. (Anvil Books).

Commager, Henry S. (ed.), *America in Perspective* (abridged). New York: New American Library (Mentor Books).

Commager, Henry S. (ed.), *The Era of Reform, 1830–1860.* Princeton, N. J.: D. Van Nostrand Co., Inc. (Anvil Books).

DeTocqueville, Alexis, *Democracy in America,* 2 vols. New York: Random House, Inc. (Vintage Books).

‡Frankfurter, Marion D. and Gardner Jackson (eds.), *Letters of Sacco and Vanzetti.* New York: E. P. Dutton & Co., Inc. (Everyman Paperbacks).

Hesseltine, William B. (ed.), *Third Party Movements in the United States.* Princeton, N. J.: D. Van Nostrand Co., Inc. (Anvil Books).

Hofstadter, Richard (ed.), *The Progressive Movement, 1900–1915.* Prentice-Hall, Inc. (Spectrum Books).

Kimball, William J. (ed.), *Richmond in Time of War.* Boston: Houghton Mifflin Co.

Kirwan, Albert D. (ed.), *Confederacy.* New York: World Publishing Co. (Meridian Books).

‡Leuchtenberg, William E. (ed.), *Theodore Roosevelt: The New Nationalism.* Englewood Cliffs, N. J.: Prentice-Hall, Inc. (Spectrum Books).

‡Leuchtenberg, William E. (ed.), *Woodrow Wilson: The New Freedom.* Englewood Cliffs, N. J.: Prentice-Hall, Inc. (Spectrum Books).

Lippmann, Walter (ed.), *Drift and Mastery: An Attempt to Diagnose the Current Unrest.* Englewood Cliffs, N. J.: Prentice-Hall, Inc. (Spectrum Books).

Logan, Rayford W. (ed.), *The Negro in the United States: A Brief History.* Princeton, N. J.: D. Van Nostrand Co., Inc. (Anvil Books).

McKitrick, Eric L. (ed.), *Slavery Defended: The Views of the Old South.* Englewood Cliffs, N. J.: Prentice-Hall, Inc. (Spectrum Books).

Miller, William (ed.), *Men in Business: Essays on the Historical Role of the Entrepreneur.* New York: Harper & Row (Torchbooks).

Morris, Richard B. (ed.), *The Basic Ideas of Alexander Hamilton.* New York: Washington Square Press.

‡Pritchett, C. Herman (ed.), *American Constitutional Issues.* New York: McGraw-Hill Book Co.

‡Probst, George E. (ed.), *The Happy Republic: A Reader in Tocqueville's America.* New York: Harper & Row.

Rauch, Basil D. (ed.), *Franklin D. Roosevelt: Selected Speeches, Messages, Press Conferences, and Letters.* New York: Holt, Rinehart & Winston, Inc.

Reed, V. B. and J. D. Williams (eds.), *The Case of Aaron Burr.* Boston: Houghton Mifflin Co.

Shannon, David A. (ed.), *The Great Depression.* Englewood Cliffs, N. J.: Prentice-Hall, Inc. (Spectrum Books).

Still, Bayrd (ed.), *The West: Collection of Primary Sources on the American Westward Expansion.* G. P. Putnam's Sons (Capricorn Books).

Twelve Southerners, *I'll Take My Stand: The South and the Agrarian Tradition*. New York: Harper & Row (Torchbooks).

Williams, T. Harry (ed.), *Abraham Lincoln: Selected Speeches, Messages and Letters*. New York: Holt, Rinehart & Winston.

Wish, Harvey (ed.), *Ante-Bellum* (essays of Hinton R. Helper and George Fitzhugh). New York: G. P. Putnam's Sons (Capricorn Books).

Wish, Harvey (ed.), *The Slave States Before the Civil War*. New York: G. P. Putnam's Sons (Capricorn Books).

GENERAL COLLECTIONS OF INTERPRETATIONS

Amherst "Problems in American Civilization" series. Boston: D. C. Heath & Co.

Puritanism in Early America, G. M. Waller (ed.)

*Causes of the American Revolution, J. C. Wahlke (ed.)

*The Declaration of Independence and the Constitution, E. Latham (ed.)

Benjamin Franklin and the American Character, C. L. Sanford (ed.)

Hamilton and the National Debt, G. R. Taylor (ed.)

The Turner Thesis Concerning the Role of the Frontier in American History, G. R. Taylor (ed.)

*Jackson Versus Biddle: Struggle over the Second Bank of the U. S., G. R. Taylor (ed.)

The Transcendentalist Revolt Against Materialism, G. E. Whicher (ed.)

The Compromise of 1850, E. C. Rozwenc (ed.)

*Causes of the American Civil War, E. C. Rozwenc (ed.)

*Slavery as a Cause of the Civil War, E. C. Rozwenc (ed.)

Reconstruction in the South, E. C. Rozwenc (ed.)

*Democracy and the Gospel of Wealth, G. Kennedy (ed.)

John D. Rockefeller: Robber Baron or Industrial Statesman?, E. Latham (ed.)

The Pullman Boycott of 1894: The Problem of Federal Intervention, C. E. Warne (ed.)

William Jennings Bryan and the Campaign of 1896, G. F. Whicher (ed.)

*American Imperialism in 1898, T. P. Greene (ed.)

Roosevelt, Wilson, and the Trusts, E. C. Rozwenc (ed.)

Pragmatism and American Culture, G. Kennedy (ed.)

Wilson at Versailles, T. P. Greene (ed.)

Industry-Wide Collective Bargaining: Promise or Menace?, C. E. Warne (ed.)

The New Deal: Revolution or Evolution?, E. C. Rozwenc (ed.)

Franklin D. Roosevelt and the Supreme Court, A. H. Cope and F. Krinsky (eds.)

Pearl Harbor: Roosevelt and the Coming of the War, G. M. Waller (ed.)

The Yalta Conference, R. F. Fenno (ed.)

Education for Democracy: The Debate over the Report of the President's Commission on Higher Education, G. Kennedy (ed.)

Immigration: An American Dilemma, B. M. Ziegler (ed.)

Evolution and Religion: The Conflict Between Science and Theology in Modern America, G. Kennedy (ed.)

Loyalty in a Democratic State, J. Wahlke (ed.)

Desegregation and the Supreme Court, B. M. Ziegler (ed.)

Booker T. Washington and His Critics: The Problem of Negro Leadership, H. Hawkins (ed.)

*Eisenstadt, Abraham S. (ed.), *American History: Recent Interpretations.* Vol. I: To 1877. Vol. II: Since 1865. New York: Thomas Y. Crowell.

*Fine, Sidney and Gerald S. Brown (eds.), *The American Past: Conflicting Interpretations of the Great Issues.* 2 vols. New York: Macmillan.

Fine, Sidney (ed.), *Recent America: Conflicting Interpretations of the Great Issues.* New York: Macmillan. (Since 1900 and basically the same as Volume II of *The American Past.*)

OVERVIEWS OF INTERPRETATIONS

American Historical Association, Service Center for Teachers of History series. More than forty titles in both world and American history, but only those pamphlets relating to the study of interpretations in American history are listed, in the order of their publication.

New Interpretations in American Foreign Policy

The South in American History

Civil War and Reconstruction

The American Revolution: A Review of Changing Interpretations

The American Frontier

Jacksonian Democracy

The Progressive Movement

1900–1920: Recent Ideas and New Literature

New Interpretations of American Colonial History

The New Deal in Historical Perspective

The Far West in American History

American Intervention: 1917–1941

United States History: A Bridge to the World of Ideas

Normalcy and Reaction, 1921–1933

The Age of Reinterpretation

Civil Rights: Retrospect and Prospects

Military History

The Federal Age, 1789–1829: America in the Process of Becoming

Money Grows Up in American History

The Founding Fathers: Young Men of the Revolution

‡Higham, John (ed.), *The Reconstruction of American History.* New York:

Harper & Row (Torchbooks). Includes "The Puritan Strain," "The Revolutionary Era," "The Changing West," "The Age of the Common Man," "Disunion and Reunion," "The Working Class," "The Realm of Wealth," "The Progressive Tradition," "Emergence to World Power," "The Quest for the National Character."

SPECIAL AREAS INTERPRETATIONS

Bugg, James L., Jr. (ed.), *Jacksonian Democracy: Myth or Reality?* New York: Holt, Rinehart & Winston, Inc.

Grebstein, Sheldon N. (ed.), *Monkey Trial.* Boston: Houghton Mifflin Co.

Handlin, Oscar (ed.), *Immigration as a Factor in American History.* Englewood Cliffs, N. J.: Prentice-Hall, Inc. (Spectrum Books).

‡Kallich, Martin and A. MacLeish (eds.), *The American Revolution Through British Eyes.* New York: Harper & Row.

Keller, Morton (ed.), *The New Deal: What Was It?* New York: Holt, Rinehart & Winston.

Satin, Joseph (ed.), *The 1950's: America's "Placid" Decade.* Boston: Houghton Mifflin Co.

FOREIGN AFFAIRS: DOCUMENTS, READINGS, AND INTERPRETATIONS

Barck, Oscar T., Jr. (ed.), *America in the World: 20th Century History in Documents.* New York: World Publishing Co. (Meridian Books).

Brockway, Thomas P. (ed.), *Basic Documents in United States Foreign Policy.* Princeton, N. J.: D. Van Nostrand Co., Inc. (Anvil Books).

Divine, Robert A. (ed.), *American Foreign Policy: A Documentary History.* New York: World Publishing Co. (Meridian Books).

‡Goldwin, Robert A. and G. Stourzh (ed.), *Readings in American Foreign Policy.* New York: Oxford University Press.

Graebner, Norman A. (ed.), *Cold War Diplomacy, American Foreign Policy 1945–1960.* Princeton, N. J.: D. Van Nostrand Co. (Anvil Books).

Keen, Benjamin (ed.), *Readings in Latin-American Civilization.* Boston: Houghton Mifflin Co.

Perkins, Bradford (ed.), *The Causes of the War of 1812: National Honor or National Interest.* New York: Holt, Rinehart & Winston, Inc.

Talman, James J. (ed.), *Basic Documents in Canadian History.* Princeton, N. J.: D. Van Nostrand Co., Inc. (Anvil Books).

GOVERNMENT: DOCUMENTS, READINGS, AND INTERPRETATIONS

‡Christenson, Reo M. and R. O. McWilliams (eds.), *Voice of the People: Readings in Public Opinion and Propaganda.* New York: McGraw-Hill Book Co.

Commager, Henry S. (ed.), *Selections From the Federalist*. New York: Appleton-Century-Crofts.

‡Dixon, Robert G., Jr., and E. Plischke, *American Government: Basic Documents and Materials*. Princeton, N. J.: Van Nostrand Co., Inc.

Rossiter, Clinton (ed.), *The Federalist Papers, Hamilton, Madison, Jay*. New York: New American Library (Mentor Books).

Scott, Andrew and E. Wallace (eds.), *Politics, U.S.A.: Cases in the American Democratic Process*. New York: Macmillan.

Swisher, Carl B. (ed.), *Historic Decisions of the Supreme Court*. Princeton, N. J.: D. Van Nostrand Co., Inc. (Anvil Books).

‡Westin, Alan F. (ed.), *Charles A. Beard: The Supreme Court and the Constitution*. Englewood Cliffs, N. J.: Prentice-Hall, Inc. (Spectrum Books).

ECONOMIC HISTORY AND ECONOMICS: DOCUMENTS, READINGS, AND INTERPRETATIONS

Hacker, Louis M. (ed.), *American Capitalism: Its Promise and Accomplishment*. Princeton, N. J.: D. Van Nostrand Co., Inc. (Anvil Books).

Hacker, Louis M. (ed.), *Major Documents in American Economic History*. Princeton, N. J.: D. Van Nostrand Co., Inc. (Anvil Books).

Harlan, H. C. (ed.), *Readings in Economics and Politics*. New York: Oxford University Press.

Harriss, C. Lowell (ed.), *Selected Readings in Economics*. Englewood Cliffs, N. J.: Prentice-Hall, Inc.

Letwin, William L. (ed.), *Documentary History of American Economic Policy Since 1789*. New York: W. W. Norton & Co.

‡Manning, Thomas, and D. Potter, *et. al.* (eds.), *Government and the American Economy: 1870–Present*. New York: Holt, Rinehart & Winston. 10 separate pamphlets.

Appendix B: Unit-Related Readings in Paperback

GENERAL AMERICAN HISTORY

Beard, Charles A., *The Economic Basis of Politics and Related Writings.* New York: Random House, Inc. (Vintage Books).

Boorstin, Daniel, *The Genius of American Politics.* Chicago: University of Chicago Press (Phoenix Books).

Brogan, Dennis W., *Politics in America.* New York: Doubleday & Co., Inc. (Anchor Books).

Degler, Carl N., *Out of Our Past: The Forces That Shaped Modern America.* New York: Harper & Row (Colophon Books).

Hansen, Marcus L. *The Atlantic Migration, 1607–1860.* New York: Harper & Row (Torchbooks).

†Hartz, Louis, *The Liberal Tradition in America: An Interpretation of American Political Thought Since the Revolution.* New York: Harcourt, Brace & World (Harvest Books).

†Hofstadter, Richard, *The American Political Tradition.* New York: Random House, Inc. (Vintage Books).

Morris, Richard B., *Great Presidential Decisions.* New York: Fawcett World Library (Premier Books).

†Parrington, Vernon L., *Main Currents in American Thought.* Vol. I. *The Colonial Mind 1620–1800.* Vol. II. *The Romantic Revolution in America 1800–1860.* Vol. III. *The Beginnings of Critical Realism 1860–1920.* New York: Harcourt, Brace & World (Harvest Books).

†Rossiter, Clinton, *The American Presidency.* New York: New American Library (Mentor Books).

Tyler, Alice F., *Freedom's Ferment.* New York: Harper & Row (Torchbooks).

Vinmont, R. B., *Our Presidents at a Glance: Washington Through Johnson.* Menlo Park, Cal.: Pacific Coast Publishers.

†Wish, Harvey (ed.), *American Historians: A Selection.* New York: Oxford University Press.

TOPIC I: THE AMERICAN REVOLUTION: STRUGGLE AGAINST TYRANNY OR UNFORTUNATE ACCIDENT?

†‡Adams, Randolph G., *Political Ideas of the American Revolution*. New York: Barnes and Noble.

Alden, John R., *The American Revolution, 1775–1783*. New York: Harper & Row (Torchbooks).

†Andrews, Charles M., *Colonial Background of the American Revolution*. New Haven, Conn.: Yale University Press.

Aptheker, Herbert, *The American Revolution, 1763–1783*. New York: International Publishers (New World Paperbacks).

Bowen, Catherine D., *John Adams and the American Revolution*. New York: Grosset & Dunlap (Universal Library).

Bridenbaugh, Carl and Jessica, *Rebels and Gentlemen: Philadelphia in the Age of Franklin*. New York: Oxford University Press (Hesperides Paperbacks).

†Brinton, Crane, *Anatomy of Revolution*. New York: Random House, Inc. (Vintage Books).

Eggleston, Edward, *The Transit of Civilization from England to America in the 17th Century*. Boston: Beacon Press.

Gentz, Frederick, *Three Revolutions Compared*. Chicago: Henry Regnery Co. (Gateway Editions).

†Gipson, Lawrence H., *The Coming of the Revolution: 1763–1775*. New York: Harper & Row (Torchbooks).

†‡Jameson, J. Franklin, *The American Revolution Considered As a Social Movement*. Boston: Beacon Press.

†Jernegan, Marcus W., *The American Colonies, 1492–1750*. Frederick Ungar.

†Knollenberg, Bernhard, *Origin of the American Revolution 1759–1766*. New York: Macmillan (Free Press Paperbacks).

†McIlwain, Charles H., *The American Revolution: A Constitutional Interpretation*. Ithaca, N. Y.: Cornell University Press.

Miller, Perry, *The New England Mind: From Colony to Province*. Boston: Beacon Press.

†Morgan, Edmund S., *Birth of the Republic, 1763–1789*, Chicago History of American Civilization. Chicago: University of Chicago Press.

Morgan, Edmund S. and Helen S., *Stamp Act Crisis: Prologue to Revolution*. New York: Macmillan (Collier Books).

Morison, Samuel E., *Intellectual Life of Colonial New England*. Ithaca, N. Y.: Cornell University Press.

Notestein, Wallace, *The English People on the Eve of Colonization, 1603–1630*. New York: Harper & Row (Torchbooks).

Rossiter, Clinton, *The First American Revolution: The American Colonies on the Eve of Independence*. New York: Harcourt, Brace & World (Harvest Books).

Schneider, Herbert, *The Puritan Mind.* Ann Arbor, Mich.: University of Michigan Press (Ann Arbor Books).

Tyler, Moses Coit, *Patrick Henry.* Ithaca, N. Y.: Cornell University Press.

Wertenbaker, T. J., *The Puritan Oligarchy.* New York: Grosset & Dunlap, Inc. (Universal Library).

TOPIC II: THE CONSTITUTION: REJECTION
OR REAFFIRMATION OF THE
DECLARATION OF INDEPENDENCE?

†Beard, Charles A., *An Economic Interpretation of the Constitution of the United States.* New York: Macmillan (Free Press Paperbacks).

Beard, Charles A., *The Enduring Federalist.* New York: Frederick Ungar.

†Becker, Carl, *The Declaration of Independence.* New York: Random House, Inc. (Vintage Books).

†Farrand, Max, *The Framing of the Constitution of the United States.* New Haven, Conn.: Yale University Press.

†Jensen, Merrill, *The Articles of Confederation: An Interpretation of the Social-Constitutional History of the American Revolution, 1774–1781.* Madison, Wis.: University of Wisconsin Press.

Larabee, Leonard, *Conservatism in Early American History.* Ithaca, N. Y.: Cornell University Press.

Miller, John C., *The Federalist Era: 1789–1801.* New York: Harper & Row (Torchbooks).

Padover, Saul K., *The Living U. S. Constitution.* New York: New American Library (Mentor Books).

‡Schachner, Nathan, *Alexander Hamilton.* New York: A. S. Barnes & Co. (Perpetua Books).

‡Schachner, Nathan, *The Founding Fathers.* New York: G. P. Putnam's Sons (Capricorn Books).

†Van Doren, Carl, *The Great Rehearsal.* New York: Viking Press, Inc. (Compass Books).

TOPIC III: JACKSONIAN DEMOCRACY:
LIBERAL TRADITION
OR CONSERVATIVE REACTION?

1. JEFFERSON

†Adams, Henry, *The United States in 1800.* Ithaca, N. Y.: Cornell University Press.

†Beloff, Max, *Thomas Jefferson and American Democracy.* New York: Macmillan (Collier Books).

Boorstin, Daniel, *The Lost World of Thomas Jefferson.* Boston: Beacon Press.

†Charles, Joseph, *The Origins of the American Party System*. New York: Harper & Row (Torchbooks).

Chinard, Gilbert, *Thomas Jefferson: the Apostle of Americanism*. Ann Arbor, Mich.: University of Michigan Press (Ann Arbor Books).

Dewey, John, *The Living Thoughts of Thomas Jefferson*. New York: Fawcett World Library (Premier Books).

‡Frothingham, O. B., *Transcendentalism in New England: A History*. New York: Harper & Row (Torchbooks).

Jefferson, Thomas, *Autobiography*. New York: G. P. Putnam's Sons (Capricorn Books).

‡Patterson, Caleb P., *The Constitutional Principles of Thomas Jefferson*. Austin, Tex.: University of Texas Press.

†Peterson, Merrill, *The Jefferson Image in the American Mind*. New York: Oxford University Press (Galaxy Books).

†Wiltse, C. W., *The Jeffersonian Tradition in American Democracy*. New York: Hill & Wang, Inc. (American Century Series).

2. JACKSON

†Benson, Lee, *The Concept of Jacksonian Democracy: New York as a Test Case*. New York: Atheneum.

Coit, Margaret L., *John C. Calhoun: American Portrait*. Boston: Houghton Mifflin Co.

Current, Richard N., *Daniel Webster and the Rise of National Conservatism*. Boston: Little, Brown & Co.

Eaton, Clement, *Henry Clay and the Art of American Politics*. Boston: Little, Brown & Co.

‡Grund, F. J., *Aristocracy in America: Jacksonian Democracy*. New York: Harper & Row (Torchbooks).

James, Marquis, *Portrait of a President, Andrew Jackson*. New York: Grosset & Dunlap, Inc. (Universal Library).

†Meyers, Marvin, *The Jacksonian Persuasion: Politics and Belief*. New York: Random House, Inc. (Vintage Books).

Schlesinger, Arthur M., Jr., *The Age of Jackson*. Boston: Little, Brown & Co.

†Van Deusen, Glyndon, *The Jacksonian Era, 1828–1848*. New York: Harper & Row (Torchbooks).

†Ward, John W., *Andrew Jackson: Symbol for an Age*. New York: Oxford University Press (Galaxy Books).

TOPIC IV: WESTWARD EXPANSION: "MANIFEST DESTINY" OR ECONOMIC IMPERIALISM?

Bakeless, John, *Lewis and Clark: Partners in Discovery*. New York: Apollo Editions.

‡Billington, Ray A., *The American Frontier*. New York: Macmillan.

De Voto, Bernard, *Course of Empire*. Boston: Houghton Mifflin Co. (Sentry Editions).

De Voto, Bernard, *Year of Decision: 1846*. Boston: Houghton Mifflin Co. (Sentry Editions).

†Faulkner, Harold U., *Politics, Reform and Expansion: 1890–1900*. New York: Harper & Row (Torchbooks).

†‡Freidel, Frank, *Splendid Little War*. New York: Dell Publishing Co.

Parkman, Francis, *The Oregon Trail*. New York: New American Library (Signet Books).

Robbins, Roy M., *Our Landed Heritage: The Public Domain, 1776–1936*. Lincoln, Neb.: University of Nebraska Press (Bison Books).

Smith, Henry N., *Virgin Land: The American West as Symbol and Myth*. New York: Random House, Inc. (Vintage Books).

Turner, Frederick J., *The Frontier in American History*. New York: Holt, Rinehart & Winston, Inc.

Webb, Walter P., *The Great Plains*. New York: Grosset & Dunlap, Inc. (Universal Library).

TOPIC V: THE CIVIL WAR: IRREPRESSIBLE OR AVOIDABLE CONFLICT?

Aptheker, Herbert, *American Negro Slave Revolts*. New York: International Publishers (New World Paperbacks).

‡Buckmaster, Henrietta, *Let My People Go: The Story of the Underground Railroad and the Abolition Movement*. Boston: Beacon Press.

Cash, W. J., *The Mind of the South*. New York: Random House, Inc. (Vintage Books).

Charnwood, Lord, *Lincoln*. New York: Simon & Schuster, Inc. (Pocket Books, Inc.).

Current, Richard N., *The Lincoln Nobody Knows*. Hill & Wang, Inc. (American Century Series).

†Donald, David, *Lincoln Reconsidered: Essays on the Civil War Era*. New York: Random House, Inc. (Vintage Books).

†Dumond, Dwight L., *Anti-Slavery Origins of the Civil War in the United States*. Ann Arbor, Mich.: University of Michigan Press (Ann Arbor Books).

†Elkins, Stanley M., *Slavery*. New York: Grosset & Dunlap, Inc. (Universal Library).

Filler, Louis, *Crusade Against Slavery: 1830–1860*. New York: Harper & Row (Torchbooks).

‡McMaster, John B., *Our House Divided*. New York: Fawcett World Library (Premier Books).

Nevins, Allan, *The Statesmanship of the Civil War*. New York: Macmillan (Collier Books).

†Nichols, Roy F., *Disruption of American Democracy*. New York: Macmillan (Free Press Paperbacks).

†Potter, David M., *Lincoln and His Party in the Secession Crisis*. New Haven, Conn.: Yale University Press.

Pressley, Thomas J., *Americans Interpret Their Civil War*. New York: Macmillan (Free Press Paperbacks).

Wheare, K. C., *Lincoln*. New York: Macmillan (Collier Books).

TOPIC VI: RECONSTRUCTION: EXPLOITATION OF THE SOUTH OR GENUINE REFORM?

†Allen, James S., *Reconstruction: The Battle for Democracy*. New York: International Publishers (New World Paperbacks).

†Bowers, Claude, *The Tragic Era: The Revolution After Lincoln*. Boston: Houghton Mifflin Co. (Sentry Editions).

Buck, Paul H., *The Road to Reunion: 1865–1900*. Boston: Little, Brown & Co.

Cash, W. J., *The Mind of the South*. New York: Random House, Inc. (Vintage Books).

DuBois, W. E. B., *Black Reconstruction in America*. New York: World Publishing Co. (Meridian Books).

†Dunning, William A., *Reconstruction, Political and Economic: 1865–1877*. New York: Harper & Row (Torchbooks).

Franklin, John H., *Reconstruction: After the Civil War*, Chicago History of American Civilization. Chicago: University of Chicago Press.

†Woodward, C. Vann, *Reunion and Reaction: The Compromise of 1877 and the End of Reconstruction*. Boston: Little, Brown & Co.

Woodward, C. Vann, *The Strange Career of Jim Crow*. New York: Oxford University Press (Galaxy Books).

TOPIC VII: THE GILDED AGE: ABANDONMENT OF MORALS OR PERIOD OF ADJUSTMENT?

†Adams, Charles F., Jr. and Henry, *Chapters of Erie*. Ithaca, N. Y.: Cornell University Press.

†Allen, Frederick L., *The Great Pierpont Morgan*. New York: Harper & Row (Perennial Library).

Beer, Thomas, *The Mauve Decade: American Life at the End of the 19th Century*. New York: Random House, Inc. (Vintage Books).

‡Burlingame, Roger, *Henry Ford*. New York: New American Library (Signet Books).

Burlingame, Roger, *Machines That Built America*. New York: New American Library (Signet Books).

Burlingame, Roger, *March of the Iron Men*. New York: Grosset & Dunlap (Universal Library).

Childs, Marquis and Douglas Cater, *Ethics in a Business Society*. New York: New American Library (Mentor Books).

Cochran, Thomas C., *American Business System: A Historical Perspective, 1900–1955*. New York: Harper & Row (Torchbooks).

†Cochran, Thomas C. and William Miller, *Age of Enterprise: A Social History of Industrial America*. New York: Harper & Row (Torchbooks).

Handlin, Oscar, *Race and Nationality in American Life*. New York: Doubleday & Co., Inc. (Anchor Books).

‡Handlin, Oscar, *The Uprooted*. New York: Grosset & Dunlap (Universal Library).

†Hays, Samuel, *The Response to Industrialism, 1885–1914*. Chicago History of American Civilization. Chicago: University of Chicago Press.

Higham, John, *Strangers in the Land: Patterns in American Nativism, 1860–1925*. New York: Atheneum.

Hofstadter, Richard, *Social Darwinism in American Thought*, Boston: Beacon Press.

†Josephson, Matthew, *Robber Barons*. New York: Harcourt, Brace & World (Harvest Books).

†Lundberg, Ferdinard, *America's Sixty Families*. New York: Citadel Press.

Lynd, Robert S. and H. M., *Middletown*. New York: Harcourt, Brace & World (Harvest Books).

Osgood, Ernest S., *Day of the Cattleman*. Chicago: University of Chicago Press (Phoenix Books).

Tawney, R. H., *Religion and the Rise of Capitalism*. New York: New American Library (Mentor Books).

Veblen, Thorstein, *Higher Learning in America*. New York: Hill & Wang, Inc. (American Century Paperbacks).

Warner, W. Lloyd and James Abeggeen, *Big Business Leaders in America*. New York: Atheneum.

TOPIC VIII: THE NEW DEAL: EVOLUTION OR REVOLUTION?

1. POPULISM

Buck, Solon, *The Granger Movement: A Study of Agricultural Organization and Its Political, Economic, and Social Manifestations, 1870–1880*. Lincoln, Neb.: University of Nebraska Press (Bison Books).

†Hicks, John D., *The Populist Revolt: A History of the Farmers' Alliance and the People's Party*. Lincoln, Neb.: University of Nebraska Press (Bison Books).

Shannon, Fred, *American Farmers' Movements*. Princeton, N. J.: D. Van Nostrand Co., Inc. (Anvil Books).

2. PROGRESSIVISM

†Aaron, Daniel, *Men of Good Hope: A Story of American Progressives*. New York: Oxford University Press (Galaxy Books).

Blum, John M., *The Republican Roosevelt*. New York: Atheneum.

Blum, John M., *Woodrow Wilson and the Politics of Morality*. Boston: Little, Brown & Co.

†Filler, Louis, *Crusaders For American Liberalism*. New York: Macmillan (Collier Books).

†Hugh-Jones, E. M., *Woodrow Wilson and American Liberalism*. New York: Macmillan (Collier Books).

LaFollette, Robert M., *LaFollette's Autobiography: A Personal Narrative of Political Experience*. Madison, Wis.: University of Wisconsin Press.

Link, Arthur S., *Woodrow Wilson and the Progressive Era, 1910–1917*. New York: Harper & Row (Torchbooks).

Mowry, George E., *The Era of Theodore Roosevelt and the Birth of Modern America, 1900–1912*. New York: Harper & Row (Torchbooks).

‡Mowry, George E., *Theodore Roosevelt and the Progressive Movement*. New York: Hill & Wang, Inc. (American Century Paperbacks).

Pringle, Henry S., *Theodore Roosevelt: A Biography*. New York: Harcourt, Brace & World (Harvest Books).

Steffens, Lincoln, *Shame of the Cities*. New York: Hill & Wang, Inc. (American Century).

3. NEW DEAL

Allen, Frederick L., *Only Yesterday*. New York: Harper & Row (Perennial Library).

Allen, Frederick L., *Since Yesterday, 1929–1939*. New York: Bantam Books, Inc.

Galbraith, John K., *The Great Crash, 1929*. Boston: Houghton Mifflin Co. (Sentry Editions).

*Goldman, Eric F., *Rendezvous With Destiny: A History of Modern American Reform* (abridged, rev. ed). New York: Random House, Inc. (Vintage Books).

Goldman, Eric F., *The Crucial Decade and After, America 1945–1960*. New York: Random House, Inc. (Vintage Books).

Gunther, John, *Roosevelt in Retrospect*. New York: Pyramid Publications, Inc.

*Hofstadter, Richard, *The Age of Reform: From Bryan to F.D.R.* New York: Random House, Inc. (Vintage Books).

Leuchtenberg, William E., *The Perils of Prosperity: 1914–1932*. Chicago: University of Chicago Press.

Leuchtenberg, William E., *Franklin D. Roosevelt and the New Deal, 1932–1940*. New York: Harper & Row (Torchbooks).

†Lubell, Samuel, *The Future of American Politics*. New York: Harper & Row (Colophon Books).

Perkins, Dexter, *The New Age of Franklin Roosevelt: 1932–1945,* Chicago History of American Civilization. Chicago: University of Chicago Press.

Sherwood, Robert E., *Roosevelt and Hopkins*. New York: Grosset & Dunlap, Inc. (Universal Library).

‡Woods, J. A., *Roosevelt and Modern America*. New York: Macmillan (Collier Books).

TOPIC IX: AMERICAN FOREIGN POLICY: ISOLATION OR COMMITMENT?

†Adler, Selig, *The Isolationist Impulse: Its 20th Century Reaction*. New York: Macmillan (Free Press Paperbacks).

†Beale, Howard K., *Theodore Roosevelt and the Rise of America to World Power*. New York: Macmillan (Collier Books).

Bemis, Samuel F., *The Diplomacy of the American Revolution*. Bloomington, Ind.: Indiana University Press.

Bemis, Samuel F., *Jay's Treaty: A Study in Commerce and Diplomacy*. New Haven, Conn.: Yale University Press.

Bemis, Samuel F., *Pinckney's Treaty: America's Advantage from Europe's Distress, 1783–1800* (rev. ed). New Haven, Conn.: Yale University Press.

‡Burtness, Paul and Warren Ober, *The Puzzle of Pearl Harbor*. New York: Harper & Row.

Dulles, Foster R., *America's Rise to World Power: 1898–1954*. New York: Harper & Row (Torchbooks).

Feis, Herbert, *The Road to Pearl Harbor*. New York: Atheneum.

Kennan, George F., *American Diplomacy, 1900–1950*. New York: New American Library (Mentor Books).

Mahan, Alfred T., *The Influence of Seapower Upon History*. New York: Hill & Wang, Inc. (American Century Paperbacks).

Morison, Elting, *Turmoil and Tradition: A Study of the Life and Times of Henry L. Stimson*. New York: Atheneum.

Perkins, Dexter, *History of the Monroe Doctrine*. Boston: Little, Brown & Co. (Atlantic-Little, Brown Paperbacks).

†Spanier, John, *American Foreign Policy Since World War II*. New York: Frederick A. Praeger, Inc.